LIFE IN HIS HANDS

A Call to Godly Surrender and
Purposeful Living

by
JILL HOLLER

SonRise Devotionals
Lighthouse Publishing of the Carolinas

LIFE IN HIS HANDS BY JILL HOLLER
Published by SonRise Devotionals,
An imprint of Lighthouse Publishing of the Carolinas
2333 Barton Oaks Dr., Raleigh, NC 27614

ISBN: 978-1-938499-58-6
Copyright © 2016 by Jill Holler
Cover design by Elaina Lee
Interior design by Karthick Srinivasan

Available in print from your local bookstore, online, or from the publisher at:
www.lighthousepublishingofthecarolinas.com.

For more information on this book and the author visit:
www.changedbyhisgrace.com.

Brought to you by the creative team at LighthousePublishingoftheCarolinas.com:
Eddie Jones, Shonda Savage, Susan Price, Elaina Lee and Cindy Sproles.

Library of Congress Cataloging-in-Publication Data
Holler, Jill
Life in His Hands / Jill Holler 1st ed.

Printed in the United States of America

PRAISE FOR *LIFE IN HIS HANDS*

AS CHRISTIANS, WE need to be reminded daily about how to live our lives for Christ; just as much, we need to be comforted and encouraged. In this collection, Jill Holler provides both the confrontation and the encouragement, not just by good ideas or personal anecdotes, but by drawing us into the Scriptures...where we can truly be fed. These brief, targeted, thoroughly biblical meditations are for the desperate and the egotistical alike--those on a journey to be more like Jesus--all of us!

~ **Dan Schoepf**,
Pastor, Calvary Church, Muscatine, Iowa

Life in His Hands is an authentic, captivating devotional that will awaken your heart to the love of Christ and the purpose he has planned for you. Just as God opened Jill's eyes to the abundant life offered only through him, you too will be able to "taste and see that the Lord is good" (Psalm 34:8). As you fix your heart and mind on the words in this book, let God fill you with the love and purpose only he can give.

~ **Mary Goossen**,
Missionary, Avant Ministries, Ipu, Ceara, Brazil

I had the privilege of being Jill's pastor during her growing up years. Jill writes from a heart overflowing with the love of the Lord and we, the readers, benefit from her words. Jill Holler writes in such a way that no matter where one is in their faith walk they will be able to glean something from these devotions.

~ **Robert E. Anderson**,
Retired EPC Pastor, Pella, Iowa

TABLE OF CONTENTS

To MY BROTHERS and sisters in Christ,

I have spent most of my life believing in God and reading His Word, yet rarely embracing the great power that lies within it. The call to write this devotional book came at a time when God opened my eyes to the futility of such living. I felt Him urging me to stop living a life that did not function on His full power and instead, embrace a life of complete submission to His will. I began to sit and be still with God, praying that He would open my eyes so that I might understand the Scriptures (Luke 24:45). As I committed myself to this, I found that His words spoke right to my heart and my circumstances. I started to see His Word as an immense treasure that, if meditated upon, could change my heart, mind, and actions, and revive my life purpose. As I put pen to paper, I found that the act of reflecting on His Word through writing was the greatest learning experience I have ever had as a believer in Christ. The words I wrote became lessons to my very own soul, ones that I needed to instill deeply into the foundation of my faith. I pray that these same truths will ring with clarity into your own hearts and souls, just as they did in mine. May God continue to bless you *with every spiritual blessing in Christ* (Ephesians 1:3) as you journey with Him.

~Jill

THE GREAT ARCHITECT

He who began a good work in you will carry it on to
completion until the day of Christ Jesus.
Philippians 1:6

GOD HAS BEGUN a good work in you. Have you recognized it and taken hold of its reality? Perhaps you have heard God's promptings within your soul to go and do something great for the advancement of His kingdom. Most likely, what God is calling you to do lies outside of the boundaries of "realistic" dreams for your life. Most often, He calls us to do things that seem beyond our abilities and to go places we aren't expecting. It is in these places that God is orchestrating His purpose in our lives.

Although we yearn for logic and thoughtful planning, God desires to take us to the places where He can take over in our weakness, places where we are completely dependent on Him because our shortcomings are so glaringly obvious. But we need not fear, because it is not we ourselves who carry out the good work that God started in us, it is God Himself. We must simply be willing vessels, who for the love of our God, will go where He leads and do what He asks.

The tight grip of control we want to maintain over our lives must be loosened. For although we desire to be the architects of our own lives, God desires to do the building Himself. He holds the blueprints for our lives, and they are more intricate and well-designed than anything we could sketch out in our own minds. If we let go of the limited plans we have for ourselves and instead, release ourselves into the loving hands of the one who *fearfully and wonderfully made* (Psalm 139:14) us, He will complete in us the work planned for us before our creation.

By faith Abraham, when called to go out to a place he would later receive as his inheritance, obeyed and went, even though he did not know where he was going. For he was looking forward to the city with foundations, whose architect and builder is God. Hebrews 11:8, 10

But He said to me, "My grace is sufficient for you, for My power is made perfect in weakness." Therefore I will boast all the more gladly about my weaknesses, so that Christ's power may rest on me. 2 Corinthians 12:9

For we are God's handiwork, created in Christ Jesus to do good works, which God prepared in advance for us to do. Ephesians 2:10

WHISPERS OF DOUBT

Are You the one who is to come, or should we expect someone else? Matthew 11:3

LOCKED IN A dark, damp prison cell, after such hope had appeared before his eyes, John the Baptist was left to question the truth of what he had seen. Images of heaven's glory shining down upon Jesus in the Jordan River were now replaced with the dark shadows that covered the prison walls. The surreal voice proclaiming, *This is my Son, whom I love* (Matthew 3:17), was now drowned out by voices of doubt whispering in John's mind. Was Jesus really the one for whom he had prepared the way? Or could he have been mistaken?

Similar voices want to whisper words of doubt into our own minds as we journey with the Lord. As He leads us to places we are not expecting, we frantically look around, proclaiming, "Certainly, this can't be part of the plan!" Just as John may have created his own glorious visions of Jesus' kingdom and the role he would play in it, we too enjoy creating our own visions of our roles in God's unfolding plan. But when those visions are confronted with a differing reality, we retreat to our doubts, disregarding the overwhelming evidence of the amazing, miraculous things He has done in our lives.

God had blessed John the Baptist with remarkable

evidence that Jesus was His Son. When John first saw Jesus on the day of His baptism, he was so taken aback at the earthly presence of the Son of God that he proclaimed, *Look, the Lamb of God, who takes away the sin of the world!* (John 1:29). He also witnessed God's Spirit descending like a dove on Jesus and heard God's voice from heaven calling Jesus His son.

But sometimes, in our distress or confusion, we can focus only on the circumstances that surround us. And the evidence that was once so alive in our hearts can slowly fade away. Our mind tries to overtake our spirit, prompting us to doubt the truth instead of cling to it. At times like these, we must pray that the Holy Spirit will come to life inside of us, confirming the truth and reality of Jesus Christ to our souls. He will not cease to be God's Advocate for truth, even when everything else, including ourselves, fails. As His Spirit testifies to ours, our hope can once again resurge, and we can become witnesses for truth to the world around us.

John replied in the words of Isaiah the prophet, "I am the voice of one calling in the wilderness, 'Make straight the way for the Lord.'" John 1:23

As soon as Jesus was baptized, He went up out of the water. At that moment, heaven was opened, and He saw the Spirit of God descending like a dove and alighting on Him. And a voice from heaven said, "This is My Son, whom I love; with Him I am well pleased."
Matthew 3:16-17

When the Advocate comes, whom I will send to you from the Father—the Spirit of truth ... He will testify about Me. John 15:26

The Spirit Himself testifies with our spirit that we are God's children.
Romans 8:16

UNSHAKEABLE

*"The mountains may depart and the hills be removed,
but My steadfast love shall not depart from you, and My
covenant of peace shall not be removed," says the* LORD
who has compassion on you. Isaiah 54:10 (ESV)

AS THE YEARS pass and you see the landscape of your life changing, altering in ways that you did not expect, your heart can be quieted by these simple truths: that the steadfast love of the Lord will never leave you and His peace will never be removed. His faithfulness has become His greatest gift to you, and His compassion is a treasure to your soul. No matter what you face, you can humbly proclaim, *It is well with my soul.*

Nothing in this world can bring this confidence to our souls, for *the world is passing away along with its desires* (1 John 2:17 ESV). Every shakable thing, from the mountains and the hills to the empires we build for ourselves, will not stand forever. All that is temporary will crumble away, leaving only what remains: a kingdom of God that cannot be shaken. What confidence we can have to go forth into the world, with God's love, peace, and compassion leading us in victory over the ways of this world.

The Word of God itself is the solid foundation for knowing that this victory is ours. As Jesus Christ Himself stated, *Heaven and earth will pass away, but My words will never pass away* (Matthew 24:35). When we take hold of our Bible, the very essence of the unshakeable is resting in our hands. When we turn to it and meditate upon it, we fix our hearts and minds upon that which does not fade away. Even if all else around us comes tumbling down, we will be able to stand, heirs to an everlasting kingdom built on the steadfast love of the Lord.

The steadfast love of the Lord *never ceases; His mercies never come to an end; they are new every morning; great is Your faithfulness.*
Lamentations 3:22-23 (ESV)

The words "once more" indicate the removing of what can be shaken—that is, created things—so that what cannot be shaken may remain. Therefore, since we are receiving a kingdom that cannot be shaken, let us be thankful, and so worship God acceptably with reverence and awe. Hebrews 12:27-28

Therefore everyone who hears these words of mine and puts them into practice is like a wise man who built his house on the rock. Matthew 7:24

THE PEACE OF THE LORD

You will go out in joy and be led forth in peace; the mountains and hills will burst into song before you, and all the trees of the field will clap their hands.
Isaiah 55:12

THE PEACE OF the Lord surrounds you in the calm, rustling breeze of spring; it comforts you with the crickets' song of summer. It dances down upon you in the falling leaves of autumn and blankets you in the winter with the softly falling snow. In a world that offers so much chaos and weariness, God blesses us with the beauty of His creation in order to remind us that His peace still rules. Even in the midst of our trials, we will be able to *taste and see that the Lord is good* (Psalm 34:8).

The Lord's glory is shown in His creation, *and He has compassion on all He has made* (Psalm 145:9). When we cannot see beyond the trouble that surrounds us, we must widen our view to see how His mercy is displayed over our world, and we will surely find it. If we cast our eyes up from the dark place we are in to see the glorious sunshine of the day, our souls will be comforted by the knowledge that there is still light in the world. And even if storms rumble across the sky and the rain falls upon us, we can witness His mercy as He blesses a dry and thirsty land.

The touches of His mercy lie within the quietness of the morning after a sleepless night of worry and desperation, where we find that our mercies—just like His—are renewed for a brand new day. His peace settles into our hearts when we look up at the night sky filled with His starry lights, and we know that the One who is in control over everything is the One we call Savior and Friend.

Nothing in our human-constructed world offers peace, only a counterfeit form of it that never delivers. When we get entrenched in the strife of this world and cannot draw forth praise from our own lips, we can look to God's great creation as our example: *The heavens declare the glory of God; the skies proclaim the work of His hands. Day after day they pour forth speech... their voice goes out into all the earth, their words to the ends of the world* (Psalm 19:1-4). Let us too find peace in proclaiming His goodness! May our voices of praise go *out into all the earth.*

Because of the LORD's great love we are not consumed, for His compassions never fail. They are new every morning; great is Your faithfulness.
Lamentations 3:22-23

For since the creation of the world, God's invisible qualities—His eternal power and divine nature—have been clearly seen, being understood from what has been made, so that people are without excuse. Romans 1:20

He makes me lie down in green pastures, He leads me beside quiet waters, He refreshes my soul. Psalm 23:2-3

MASTER PLANNER

"For I know the plans I have for you," declares the LORD,
"plans to prosper you and not to harm you, plans to give
you hope and a future." Jeremiah 29:11

ALTHOUGH GOD KNOWS the specific plans that He has for our lives, we do not. However, we wish God's plans could be presented to us in a detailed instruction manual so that each day, we could follow it in simple, mapped-out steps. In our minds, we try to predict the ungovernable future, but the uncertainty we find causes us to be filled with anxiety and tension. As we walk through life, we question whether or not we are on the right path, and we silently wonder if God really does have plans that will *give [us] hope and a future.*

This is when we must remember that no matter how we view the circumstances of life, God's ways are vastly higher than ours, and His plans are greater and much more comprehensive than we can imagine. When Job and his friends tried to figure out why Job had to go through such extreme hardship, God rebuked them for trying to use their own wisdom to assess the situation. He demanded, *Who is this that questions My wisdom with such ignorant words?* (Job 38:2 NLT). The one who determined the measurements of the earth and set the limits of the sea is completely worthy of measuring out our steps too.

Although we may desire a mapped-out plan with logic as our guide, God desires for our faith in Him to be our guide. Within His wisdom lie the keys to a future that is filled with hope and goodness, a future that goes beyond our human mindset and into the mystery of God's amazing intellect. We can find peace and assurance knowing that God Himself made specific, complex plans for us, and He can effortlessly stitch them into our lives to work out His wonderful plan.

Trust in the LORD with all your heart and lean not on your own understanding; in all your ways submit to Him, and He will make your paths straight.
Proverbs 3:5-6

Where were you when I laid the foundations of the earth? Tell Me, if you know so much. Job 38:4 (NLT)

Who kept the sea inside its boundaries as it burst from the womb? Job 38:8 (NLT)

BY FAITH

By faith Abraham, when called to go to a place he would later receive as his inheritance, obeyed and went, even though he did not know where he was going.
Hebrews 11:8

FAITH IS THE only way to arrive at the place where God has called you, since the destination is never revealed at the outset of the journey. Only through faith can you submit to the kind of radical obedience that says "yes" to plans you don't understand and "no" to ones that seem so logical. For Abraham, it would have been quite rational to live out his life in the land where he was, a place that was familiar and comfortable. However, God did not call Abraham to a life of predictability; He called him to a life of uncertainty that began with uprooting his family and heading out to an unknown destination. Only there would he find his God-ordained purpose and fulfill the destiny to which he was called, one that would result in a great blessing upon the entire world.

Our lives of purpose begin with that same step of faith that requires us to set aside logic and journey to the places we would never venture to on our own. There, God will train us to rely completely on Him as we face our own weaknesses and walk toward the unknown. As He leads us away from our own self-reliance and into a place of total trust in Him, He leads us closer to becoming the person He has destined us to be. He designed each of us to glorify His name and become a blessing to those around us, just as He did through Abraham. And just like this man of great faith, we must listen to and obey the One who calls us, shutting out the other voices that try to dissuade us from following Him.

People will undoubtedly question our logic and even criticize or mock us as we journey down a road led by an unseen guide. However, the beauty of faith is that it empowers us to stop listening to the multitude of voices that tell us the path we are taking is foolish and illogical. It quenches our desire to please everyone around us and instead emboldens our hearts to love and please only Him. With God, we are free to follow the voice of the *One whose understanding has no limit* (Psalm 147:5) and whose ways are vastly higher than our own (Isaiah 55:9). Only with a God like this can we step out in complete, unyielding faith!

Now faith is confidence in what we hope for and assurance about what we do not see. This is what the ancients were commended for. Hebrews 11:1-2

And through your offspring all nations on earth will be blessed, because you have obeyed Me. Genesis 22:18

When my spirit faints within me, You know my way.
Psalm 142:3

LUSTS OF THE WORLD

For everything that belongs to the world—the lust of the flesh, the lust of the eyes, and the pride in one's lifestyle— is not from the Father, but is from the world. And the world with its lust is passing away, but the one who does God's will remains forever. 1 John 2:16-17 (HCSB)

HOW DESPERATELY OUR arms want to reach out and grab ahold of all that is passing away! The things of this world call out to us with their false promises, tempting us to believe only in the things we can see. As we look at the material world around us, we are drawn to its enticing beauty, and we long to embrace the power and prestige that will elevate us to a higher level. As we set our eyes upon what other people have, our hearts begin to yearn for those things above all else. In the midst of such deception, our tunnel vision prevents us from seeing that all of it is merely a facade, a mirage that is here for a moment and then gone.

If we base our lives on such things, we unwisely build for ourselves an empire with no solid foundation. Just like people running excitedly toward a beautiful oasis in the middle of a desert, we arrive anxiously, only to find that there is nothing there at all. Everything we had placed our hope in vanishes quickly before our eyes. So it will be at the end of our lives if we look for those things to save us and find in utter shock that none of it mattered, not even in the least. All that was real and eternal had been traded in cheaply for the values of the world, for things that do not last.

The draw of this temptation, although so foolish, can be very convincing to our selfish, prideful hearts. Left to our own instincts, we are quick to trade in God's will for our own. Only through a mind controlled by His Spirit can we conquer the giants of the world that try to gain victory over us. Let us pray earnestly to God as the psalmist did: *Incline my heart to Your testimonies, and not to selfish gain! Turn my eyes from looking at worthless things; and give me life in Your ways* (Psalm 119:36-37 ESV). Let us see the things of this world through the value system of God's eyes and appraise them as He would. Then let us assess the value of a life lived in complete submission to His will and be amazed at its immense greatness!

Do not lay up for yourselves treasures on earth, where moth and rust destroy and where thieves break in and steal, but lay up for yourselves treasures in heaven ...
Matthew 6:19-20 (ESV)

Then He said to them, "Watch out! Be on your guard against all kinds of greed; life does not consist in an abundance of possessions." Luke 12:15

The mind governed by the flesh is death, but the mind governed by the Spirit is life and peace. Romans 8:6

FOLLOW ME

When Peter saw him [John], he said to Jesus, "Lord, what about this man?" Jesus said to him, "If it is My will that he remain until I come, what is that to you? You follow Me!" John 21:21-22 (ESV)

KEEP YOUR EYES on Jesus as you live out your purpose on this earth. Don't shift your focus to other believers in order to assess the plans God has for them. In doing so, you may unwittingly begin to compare your callings and formulate judgments about them. A resentful spirit can arise when you determine that someone else has a worthier calling than you or that your plan is filled with more hardships. These types of perceptions are destructive because they set us against other believers and shift our focus from God to ourselves.

Peter encountered this mindset as he struggled with his own calling and those of the people around him. Before his ascension, Jesus called Peter to be a shepherd to God's people, but also to face a death that would glorify God. As Peter struggled with this, he looked to his fellow disciple John and asked Jesus, *Lord, what about this man?* Jesus' response was firm: *If it is My will that he remain until I come, what is that to you? You follow Me!*

May those three words, *You follow Me,* become the sole focus of our calling. For whatever the road God calls us to walk upon, that is the one in which we can glorify Him! Only there will we find our purpose in life and our place in His story, just as Peter did. Peter learned from the rebuke of Jesus to follow Him, no matter what anyone else was required to do. He fulfilled God's calling on his life and became a testimony of God's grace and power to countless generations of believers. To achieve the same, we simply must answer the call, *Follow Me.*

Then Jesus said His disciples, "Whoever wants to be My disciple must deny themselves and take up their cross and follow Me." Matthew 16:24

"Come follow Me," Jesus said, "and I will send you out to fish for people." Matthew 4:19

And we know that in all things God works for the good of those who love Him, who have been called according to His purpose. Romans 8:28

WHERE IS YOUR GOD?

My tears have been my food day and night,
while people say to me all day long,
"Where is your God?" Psalm 42:3

HAVE YOU EVER been taunted by the enemy? Have the people or circumstances in your world crowded in upon you, smothering you with their disbelief? If so, the weight of their oppression can bear heavily upon you, leaving you feeling too weak to fight off *the powers of this dark world* (Ephesians 6:12). In your despair, tears well up inside of you, weakening you by the moment, prompting you to cling to fear. But take heart, God's Spirit can revive hope within you, even as you are surrounded by the enemy.

At times like these, we must ask God to open our eyes to see the vast forces of His goodness that surround and cover us. Just as God allowed Elisha's servant to see and be comforted by *the hills full of horses and chariots of fire all around Elisha* (2 Kings 6:17), we too can find our refuge in God's protection over our lives. In Him, we are under a covering that the enemy cannot touch. And although those around us may taunt, "Where is your God?" we can hold fast to the knowledge that He is right there with us.

The loud voices of the world want to overpower the

quiet, still voice of God that says He will never leave us, even as we face the powers of darkness. The truth remains, however, that *neither death nor life, neither angels nor demons ... nor anything else in all creation, will be able to separate us from the love of God that is in Christ Jesus our Lord* (Romans 8:38-39). Even if we travel to distant parts of the earth or sink low in the depths of our sorrow, the presence of the Lord will go with us and strengthen us in our greatest time of need.

For our struggle is not against flesh and blood, but against evil rulers, against the authorities, against the powers of this dark world and against the spiritual forces of evil in the heavenly realms. Ephesians 6:12

And Elisha prayed, "Open his eyes, LORD, so that he may see." Then the LORD opened the servant's eyes, and he looked and saw the hills full of horses and chariots of fire all around Elisha. 2 Kings 6:17

Where can I go from Your Spirit?
Where can I flee from Your presence?
If I go up to the heavens, You are there;
if I make my bed in the depths, You are there.
If I rise on the wings of the dawn,
if I settle on the far side of the sea,
even there Your hand will guide me,
Your right hand will hold me fast.
Psalm 139:7-10

THE PURPOSE OF PERSEVERANCE

You have persevered and have endured hardships for My name, and have not grown weary. Revelation 2:3

KEEP MOVING FORWARD. In spite of the obstacles you see and the words of discouragement you hear, keep pressing on. God has called you to move forward toward a goal that only He fully realizes, but He wants you to keep stepping out in faith. Some days that might mean driving your feet harder into the ground and pressing your head against the driving wind. But God calls you to follow Him, no matter the circumstances. God is faithful to bring you through hardships to reach the goal, but you must be willing to persevere.

Without enduring the testing of our faith, we cannot become who God desires us to be: *mature and complete, not lacking anything* (James 1:4). Instead, we will remain like *infants, tossed back and forth by the waves, blown here and there by every wind of teaching and by the cunning and craftiness of people in their deceitful scheming* (Ephesians 4:14). God cannot use us for His great purposes if we are likely to fall prey to the schemes and false teachings of those around us. But He will be able to use us if we are able to stand firm in our faith. Because of this, God chooses to train us up to maturity through trials and hardships, so that we can go forth in the purpose He has called us to.

This type of training does not appeal to many of us, however, for most often, we can only see the suffering of the moment, not the end result. We want to speed past the difficulties that refine our faith and somehow arrive victoriously on the other side, perfected and pure. Nevertheless, there are no shortcuts that lead to a place of true maturity and dependence upon the Lord, for our struggles are what drive us there. Each experience in suffering builds our character and confirms the life of Christ in us, for we are *co-heirs with Christ, if indeed we share in His sufferings* (Romans 8:17). Therefore, let us rejoice when we face *trials of many kinds* (James 1:2), for through them, God is shaping us more perfectly into the likeness of His Son. And that is exactly what we are called to be.

Consider it pure joy, my brothers and sisters, whenever you face trials of many kinds, because you know that the testing of your faith produces perseverance. Let perseverance finish its work so that you may be mature and complete, not lacking anything. James 1:2-4

Not only so, but we also glory in our sufferings, because we know that suffering produces perseverance; perseverance, character; and character, hope.
Romans 5:3-4

See, I have refined you, though not as silver; I have tested you in the furnace of affliction. Isaiah 48:10-11

FOLLOWING JESUS

*Then a teacher of the law came up to Him and said,
"Teacher, I will follow You wherever You go." Jesus
replied, "Foxes have dens, and birds have nests, but the
Son of Man has no place to lay His head."*
Matthew 8:19-20

As you step out to follow Jesus where He leads you,
don't cling tightly to what makes you feel secure. This
goes against our nature because our heart desires what
is safe and predictable. We want to be nestled in the
comfort of everything familiar and unthreatening,
not faced with the uncertainty of what lies around an
unknown corner. However, if we surrender to the power
of our insecurities, we may never get to the place God
wants us to go, and we will miss out on the amazing
journey He has planned for us.

Those who followed Jesus when He walked on this
earth had futures filled with many uncertainties. Where
would they sleep? What would they eat? Where would
they be tomorrow or in a few months? However, those
who let go of all they knew, and instead trusted in
Jesus, participated in the greatest journey this earth has
ever witnessed. Sometimes, their days were filled with
hardships and seemingly impossible circumstances, but
they were also filled with perfect purpose, joy, and hope

as they embarked upon an unstoppable mission led by the greatest guide.

God wants us to embrace the journey He has planned for us too, even as we face the unknown. It is there that we will find our great purpose and our great joy. It is there we will come alive in ways we never have and will rise to challenges that we could never conquer on our own. When we step out in faith, God will reach out to sustain and empower us with *the same mighty power that raised Christ from the dead* (Ephesians 1:19-20 NLT), so that we can accomplish the amazing works He has planned for us. Therefore, in the face of such great knowledge, *let us throw off everything that hinders ... and let us run with perseverance the race marked out for us* (Hebrews 12:1). Let us confidently proclaim, *I will follow You wherever You go!*

Therefore, since we are surrounded by such a great cloud of witnesses, let us throw off everything that hinders and the sin that so easily entangles. And let us run with perseverance the race marked out for us. Hebrews 12:1

I also pray that you will understand the incredible greatness of God's power for us who believe Him. This is the same mighty power that raised Christ from the dead and seated Him in the place of honor at God's right hand in the heavenly realms. Ephesians 1:19-20 NLT

The LORD himself goes before you and will be with you; He will never leave you nor forsake you. Do not be afraid; do not be discouraged. Deuteronomy 31:8

OUR FAITH: THE VICTORY

For everyone who has been born of God overcomes the world. And this is the victory that has overcome the world—our faith. 1 John 5:4 ESV

THE VOICES OF this world want to convince you that victory cannot be yours. They want to persuade you that there are limits to what you can do for God's glory, and that anything that goes beyond "reasonable" is foolishness. Eyes of scrutiny will be upon you as you step out in radical obedience to the Lord, following Him to places that most would not dare go on their own. People will try to sway you from such unreasonable plans and convince you that your faith has no merit. However, this is when we must draw upon our identity as overcomers through Christ and rise above the voices that try to weaken our faith.

The great deceiver of this world will try to convince us that God's Word has no power in our own lives. He will try to persuade us to believe his own words, which are filled with lies. In the quest for his own victory, Satan *roam[s] throughout the earth, going back and forth on it* (Job 1:7), looking for those whose faith he can make falter. He wants to steal the victory that is ours in Jesus Christ, but his lies are no match for a faith grounded in the truth of God's Word. We are children of God, and we will believe the truth of what our Father tells us: that *everyone who has been born of God overcomes the world* (1 John 5:4).

We are overcomers through our faith, and we are guaranteed victory over this world because of it. We must embrace this mindset as we ask God to reveal the path He wants us to take. If we do not, we will give in to the voices that tell us we could never do the things He has called us to. We will start believing the limitations set upon us, and then victory will belong to the enemy. God wants to use us in incredible ways to advance His kingdom and glorify His name, but we must believe it is possible through His great power. Let us start living as though we are *more than conquerors* (Romans 8:37) through Jesus Christ and that our faith is *the victory that has overcome the world* (1 John 5:4)!

The LORD said to Satan, "Where have you come from?"
Satan answered the LORD, "From roaming throughout
the earth, going back and forth on it." Job 2:2

Who is it that overcomes the world? Only the one who
believes that Jesus is the Son of God. 1 John 5:5

In all these things we are more than conquerors through
Him who loved us.
Romans 8:37

THE VINE AND THE BRANCHES

I am the vine; you are the branches. If you remain in Me and I in you, you will bear much fruit; apart from Me you can do nothing. John 15:5

HAS GOD CONFRONTED you with the undeniable reality that apart from Him, you can do nothing? Has He displayed the limitations and weaknesses of your human nature vividly upon the canvas of your life? If so, when faced with such knowledge, our reaction may be to close our eyes to the truth. However, recognizing how vastly inadequate we are without God is the tipping point of a life lived fully in His power. For when we come to the end of ourselves, God takes over and supplies us with all we need to live abundantly for Him.

God is the vine; we are the branches. If we stay connected to our lifeline, there is no limit to the amount of eternal fruit that we can produce for Him. Life-giving power springs up naturally from His being, and it can flow right through us to grow His kingdom here on earth. The results of remaining in Him will be a bountiful harvest that is beyond what we can imagine. In contrast, if we begin to believe that we can make it on our own and try to sustain ourselves, we will quickly see just how fruitless our efforts will become, for *no branch can bear fruit by itself* (John 15:4). Without God, our lives become withered and dry, void of the eternal.

What a great blessing it is, therefore, to realize that we can do nothing apart from Him! When we stay forever connected to the one who sustains us, we will experience true, fruitful living. Through God, the source of everything good, we can become all that He has created us to be: a blessing to those around us and servants who advance His kingdom purposes. What glory we can bring to God as we let Him work His power through us! As we make His Word the foundation of our life and our relationship with Him our greatest priority, we will produce fruit that will glorify God's name and have an eternal impact on the world around us.

If you remain in Me and My words remain in you, ask whatever you wish, and it will be done for you. John 15:7

I say to the LORD, *"You are my Lord; apart from you I have no good thing."* Psalm 16:2

In everything you do, put God first, and He will direct you and crown your efforts with success.
Proverbs 3:6 (TLB)

HIS STRENGTH, OUR WEAKNESS

I came to you in weakness with great fear and trembling. My message and my preaching were not with wise and persuasive words, but with a demonstration of the Spirit's power. 1 Corinthians 2:3-4

It is interesting that Paul came before his brothers in Christ *in weakness with great fear and trembling.* Paul had been considered a man of great pedigree, whose intellect was only surpassed by the confidence he had in it. But that was before he met Jesus Christ. That pivotal day on the road to Damascus, as Paul was blinded by heaven's light, his eyes were opened to the reality that he had not even begun to understand what true power and knowledge were. From that point on, never again would he look upon his own life with pride and self-satisfaction. For when one's life has been touched by Christ, it becomes *dead to sin, but alive to God in Christ Jesus* (Romans 6:11).

Christ had restored Paul's vision to see the truth, and in doing so, Paul came face to face with his own weakness. Just as he had to be led by the hand into Damascus, his own life would become a step-by-step journey in which he would rely completely on the hand of God to lead him. Christ's words to him became the anthem of his life: *My grace is sufficient for you, for My power is made perfect in weakness* (2 Corinthians 12:9). Because Paul embraced these words, God worked powerfully through him to make him one of the most influential servants for Christ the world has ever known.

God can work powerfully through us if we let His Spirit take over. Our own "wise and persuasive words" are not the answer. On the contrary, they actually become obstacles that hinder God's power from coming to life within us. Ceaseless striving to do things in our own strength only results in frustrated efforts without eternal results. But embracing God's power in our weakness results in God's Spirit being demonstrated through us for His glory. How miraculous that God can take weak, trembling people and turn them into vessels for His great power! Lord, let us be those people!

Therefore, my dear friends, as you have always obeyed ... continue to work out your salvation with fear and trembling, for it is God who works in you to will and to act in order to fulfill His good purpose.
Philippians 2:12-13

But God chose the foolish things of the world to shame the wise; God chose the weak things of the world to shame the strong. 1 Corinthians 1:27

As he neared Damascus on his journey, suddenly a light from heaven flashed around him. He fell to the ground and heard a voice say to him, "Saul, Saul, why do you persecute Me?" Acts 9:3-4

THE ONE WHO SUSTAINS US

*Surely God is my help; the Lord is the one
who sustains me.* Psalm 54:4

LET GOD TEACH you to rely solely on Him. Your human nature drives you to seek out other people to support and comfort you, yet their responses usually disappoint. You may question why the people you love cannot be everything you need them to be. But in all things, God has a purpose. Perhaps by displaying their limitations to you, God is trying to draw you closer to Him. God is good, and even when we feel the emptiness of imperfect human relationships, He is waiting to fill us with a love that will never fail and to build a relationship with us that will surpass anything we could ask for.

God is our refuge, the One *to which [we] can always go* (Psalm 71:3). He is our strong tower in the midst of the storms of life, the One we can cling to without the fear of rejection or indifference. People may be imperfect in giving love, but God is not. In the comfort of His shelter, we are free to be ourselves because His love is unconditional and His faithfulness is unmatched. No one on earth can be what He is. And inside each of us is a longing for something higher than what our own human relationships can supply. Our hearts call out to God, just as David's heart did: *From the ends of the earth*

I call to You, I call as my heart grows faint; lead me to the rock that is higher than I (Psalm 61:2).

Let us call out to God with our desperate, yearning hearts so that we may lean on the trusted rock of our salvation. What peace we will find as we place our lives in His hands, instead of the hands of those around us. As we bask in the perfection of God's love, we are able to release the people in our lives from supplying all of our emotional needs. We allow them to be imperfect, just as we are, and we can shower them with mercy instead of judgment. The habit of looking to God alone for our sustenance brings freedom, for we are no longer tied to the yoke of others, nor are they tied to ours. Christ died to set us free—free to rely solely upon Him.

It is for freedom that Christ has set us free.
Galatians 5:1

I love You, LORD, my strength.
The LORD is my rock, my fortress and my deliverer;
my God is my rock, in whom I take refuge,
my shield and the horn of my salvation, my stronghold.
Psalm 18:1-2

He will cover you with His feathers, and under His wings
you will find refuge; His faithfulness will be your shield
and rampart. Psalm 91:4

INTO THE HARVEST FIELD

Then He said to His disciples, "The harvest is plentiful but the workers are few. Ask the Lord of the harvest, therefore, to send out workers into His harvest field."
Matthew 9:37-38

JESUS PERSONALLY ASKED His disciples to pray for workers He could send out into the harvest field. Has God appointed you as an answer to their prayers in this generation? Have you been called to go out into the fields, which *are ripe for harvest* and *harvest a crop for eternal life* (John 4:35-36)? God could give no greater calling on your life than to participate in the harvest work for the redemption of souls. Around us is a vast sea of people living *harassed and helpless, like sheep without a shepherd* (John 4:36), and they are longing for hope. We know the answer: Jesus Christ. Are we willing to share it so that they may reap eternal life?

As believers, we did not spontaneously come to know Christ. Instead, we reaped what other Christians sowed before us. We gained eternal rewards from the work God called them to in their generations. In essence, *Others have done the hard work, and [we] have reaped the benefits of their labor* (John 4:38). Will we answer the call from God to do the same for others? Our Savior calls for harvest workers, for *the harvest is plentiful but the workers are few.* As Christians, we are qualified to go forth into the fields, for we have been saved through grace by Jesus Christ in His harvest field. Therefore, let us contribute with honor to the work from which we ourselves have been saved!

God weaves such an amazing, complex mystery throughout the generations of His people as He calls us individually, yet collectively, to contribute to the work of His redemption story. He creates plans that span infinitely across time, forging the work of past believers with those of the present and future. And at the center of it all is Jesus Christ, by whom we are sent out to gather in the harvest. As believers in this current age, we are the people whom God works through to carry out His great plan. We cannot leave it for the next generation, for what we do today will be vital to what they do tomorrow. Therefore, let us be a harvest blessing to the Lord in our time on this earth, so that God's gift of eternal life may multiply throughout the generations.

When He saw the crowds, He had compassion on them, because they were harassed and helpless, like sheep without a shepherd. Matthew 9:36

Don't you have a saying, 'It's still four months until harvest'? I tell you, open your eyes and look at the fields! They are ripe for harvest. Even now the one who reaps draws a wage and harvests a crop for eternal life, so that the sower and the reaper may be glad together. John 4:35-36

I sent you to reap what you have not worked for. Others have done the hard work, and you have reaped the benefits of their labor. John 4:38

THE ONE WHO IS WITH US

Suddenly a furious storm came up on the lake, so that
the waves swept over the boat. But Jesus was sleeping.
The disciples went and woke Him, saying, "Lord, save us!
We're going to drown!" Matthew 8:24-25

THE DARKEST DAYS of our lives are like the storm on the
sea. We feel like we've run out of hope, like there is no
way out of the darkness. We panic and cry out, "Lord,
save us!" in the midst of our fear, hoping He will do
something to rescue us. But still we feel afraid because
hidden beneath our cries is the haunting thought that
He just might not come through. We hope, but not with
confidence. We turn to Him, but only in despair, like
those grasping blindly for a lifeline. Just like the disciples
on the boat, we do not fully comprehend the power of
the One who is with us out on those stormy seas.

On the boat, Jesus asked His disciples a question
that speaks to our own hearts: *Why are you afraid, O you*
of little faith? (Matthew 8:26). This question stings our
souls because we long for great faith. However, when the
waves come crashing around us and swamp the boat we
are sitting in, we watch in panic as the water rises around
us, and we give into fear. We cry out to Jesus for help, but
only with logic ruling our minds and doubt piercing our
hearts. In our desperation, we reason, "How could God

possibly help me in this situation?" Oh, what a foolish question to ask! And it stems from the fact that we do not fully understand the power of the One who is with us.

The One who is with us is Jesus, the all-powerful creator of the universe, the Lamb of God who overcame death, and the One who controls the forces of nature with just the sound of His voice. This great power is with us as believers in Christ. But we cannot be strengthened by it if we don't believe in it. And we can't have unshakeable faith in God if we view Him only within the scope of our limited human minds. Therefore, let us see God for who He truly is: the One who has the power to take even the most impossible situations and turn them around for our good and His glory. When we ground ourselves in the truth of who God is, what great victory we can have over the power of our fears!

He replied, "You of little faith, why are you so afraid?" Then He got up and rebuked the winds and the waves, and it was completely calm. Matthew 8:26

The LORD your God is with you, the Mighty Warrior who saves. He will take great delight in you; in His love he will no longer rebuke you, but will rejoice over you with singing. Zephaniah 3:17

So do not fear, for I am with you; do not be dismayed, for I am your God. I will strengthen you and help you; I will uphold you with My righteous right hand. Isaiah 41:10

THE VALUE OF SUFFERING

Before the years of famine came, two sons were born to Joseph ... the second son he named Ephraim and said, "It is because God has made me fruitful in the land of my suffering." Genesis 41:50, 52

SOMETHING GOOD WILL be born out of our suffering. Even though we may not be able to envision how God will accomplish it, He is lovingly working in us and around us to bring a fruitful harvest to a seemingly barren land. Some days we may be *utterly burdened beyond our strength* and perhaps even *[despair] of life itself* (2 Corinthians 1:8 ESV). But just as He did in Joseph's life, God will take our suffering and turn it into a blessing. We will be able to look back at our lives and proclaim with a sincere heart, "God has made me fruitful in the land of my suffering."

As a slave and prisoner in Egypt, Joseph most likely could not comprehend the great plans God had in store for him, but God was working purposefully behind the scenes to prepare him for the role of a lifetime. Although it included much suffering, each step in Joseph's journey would lead him to become the man God had commissioned him to be: a servant of the Lord whose heart would remain humble and loyal, even when placed in a position of great glory. When the Pharaoh of

Egypt met him, he recognized that there was none other like him in all the land. He saw the hand of God upon Joseph's life and proclaimed, *Can we find anyone like this man, one in whom is the Spirit of God?* (Genesis 41:38).

What an amazing testimony this was to Joseph's role as a servant of the Lord! Yet it was a testimony born from painful times of suffering when he was forced to rely on God alone. Only through his trials and troubles was he able to *come forth as gold* (Job 23:10) and bless God's chosen people so richly. Similar blessings can flow through our own lives as we become refined through our own suffering. Through it, we learn *not [to] rely on ourselves but on God* (2 Corinthians 1:9), and we learn to embrace His vast power instead of our own limited strength. Just like with Joseph, God can use us in powerful ways as He turns our suffering into blessings and makes us fruitful beyond our abilities. Only through God do we have this great hope, and only through Him can such great abundance flow.

We went through fire and water,
but You brought us to a place of abundance.
Psalm 66:12

He knows the way that I take; when He has tested me,
I will come forth as gold.
Job 23:10

For we do not want you to be unaware, brothers, of the affliction we experienced in Asia. For we were so utterly burdened beyond our strength that we despaired of life itself. Indeed, we felt that we had received the sentence of death. But that was to make us rely not on ourselves but on God who raises the dead.
2 Corinthians 1:8-9

SWORD OF VICTORY

*The priest replied, "The sword of Goliath the Philistine,
whom you killed in the Valley of Elah, is here; it is
wrapped in a cloth behind the ephod. If you want it,
take it; there is no sword here but that one." David said,
"There is none like it; give it to me." 1 Samuel 21:9*

DAVID DID NOT go seeking Goliath's sword, but God put
it back into his hands. David was entering one of the
most tumultuous periods of his life, where death was
constantly lurking at the hands of evil King Saul. God
knew David's heart; it was filled with fear, loneliness, and
desperation. And He knew what David needed: a clear
reminder that victory is always possible with God, even
when faced with larger-than-life enemies. On the run
without any weapons, David came to a priest and asked
what he could give him. And by no mere coincidence,
the priest said he had nothing to offer but the very same
sword with which David had slain the giant.

As David set his eyes upon that sword and felt its
weight in his own hands, his heart and mind were surely
filled with the images and emotions of his first victory
in the name of the Lord Almighty. Perhaps he was swept
over with the peace and assurance that God can do
anything. Surely he was strengthened by this symbol
of God's faithfulness, which he could hold on to tightly

with his own hands. What a blessing to David, and to us, when God graces us with such reminders of our victories gained through Him! God knows we must travel down some dark roads of trials and suffering, so along the way, He gives us glimpses of His past faithfulness so that we will be able to carry on.

Even though we may feel vastly alone in our own troubles, as though *the loyal have disappeared from the human race* (Psalm 12:1), we are not left to wander this earth alone. When it appears that everyone around us has left us and *no faithful one remains* (Psalm 12:1), God wants us to know deep within our souls that He has not. He sees our troubles and knows the afflictions of our souls (Psalm 31:7 paraphrase). And in His great love for us, He will carry us through and strengthen us, just as He did with David.

Are you in the midst of trials or suffering today? Look for His strength right where you are. What glimpse of His faithfulness does He want to show you? Recall a victory from the past that only God could have given you, and cling to it tightly. Ask God to make it a treasure in your heart and a comfort to your soul, for as David said, *There is none like it.*

David said to the Philistine, "You come against me with sword and spear and javelin, but I come against you in the name of the Lord Almighty, the God of the armies of Israel, whom you have defied." 1 Samuel 17:45

I will be glad and rejoice in Your love, for You saw my affliction and knew the anguish of my soul. Psalm 31:7

As for me, I call to God, and the Lord saves me. Evening, morning and noon I cry out in distress, and He hears my voice. Psalm 55:16-17

A CALL TO OBEDIENCE

Now listen, you who say, "Today or tomorrow we will go to this or that city, spend a year there, carry on business and make money." Why, you do not even know what will happen tomorrow ... Instead, you ought to say, "If it is the Lord's will, we will live and do this or that."
James 4:13-15

GOD'S PLANS FOR us are rarely the ones that we have set in our minds. The dreams we most often form in our minds are ones that result in success and monetary gain, ones which are built upon our hard work and amazing talents. They are dreams that end with our feet up in a well-deserved vacation home, where we can finally live in leisure after years of hard work and concentrated efforts on achieving personal success. These are the dreams that the world wants us to embrace. And the prince of this world knows he can convince us rather easily to do anything for the fame of our own name.

God's plans for us are often different, however, and they have nothing to do with the fame of our name. They are summed up quite succinctly like this: if it is the Lord's will, we will remain alive and do whatever He asks (James 4:15). What clear and simple instructions! God willing, all we must do is live and obey. This is such a humbling contrast to the ways of this world, which tell us we must fight to get all we can. We are taught to make plans, conquer the world, and achieve success for ourselves. However, God makes it clear that these types of selfish ambition are not part of our job description. Instead, He simply requires that we submit to Him and serve Him with a humble heart.

When we get to the point in our lives where we can understand and accept this calling, we are closer to embracing the life that Christ has called us to. Jesus Himself provides the perfect example of living in submission to God, His father. When He walked this earth, He did not spend His time planning, scheming, or strategizing on how to be the best savior He could be. He simply listened to His father and obeyed. Even at the point of His own death, Jesus submitted completely, saying, *Not My will, but Yours be done*" (Luke 22:42). If our lives as Christians could display a fraction of the obedience Christ had, what great advances we could make for His kingdom on this earth! Let us walk in submission, as Christ did, as we answer the call to live for God and to do whatever He asks.

For in Him we live and move and have our being.
Acts 17:28

Teach me to do Your will, for You are my God; may Your good Spirit lead me on level ground. Psalm 143:10

But I gave them this command: Obey Me, and I will be your God and you will be My people. Walk in obedience to all I command you, that it may go well with you.
Jeremiah 7:23

BATTLE OF SPIRIT AND FLESH

The spirit is willing, but the flesh is weak.
Matthew 26:41

THERE IS A war raging within the souls of all believers, and it is the battle of spirit and flesh. When our spirits are soaring upon the heights of God's great power living in us, we feel unstoppable in the face of enemies and are confident in our allegiance to Christ. We may even proclaim our willingness to lay down our lives for our Savior, just as Peter did when he declared, *Even if I have to die with You, I will never disown You* (Matthew 26:35). Yet, when confronted with the circumstances that we are so certain we can conquer, our flesh becomes weak and we choose to do the very opposite of what we desire (Romans 7:15).

Great conflict surges in our hearts and minds, for as the apostle Paul stated, *[We] do not understand [our] own actions* (Romans 7:15); they are contrary to everything we believe. However, even though we are made new in Christ through our salvation, we still must walk in physical bodies on this earth. And because we live in the flesh, which *is hostile to God* (Romans 8:7), we are constantly fighting against the nature of sin within us. Just as Paul struggled with this inner conflict, we too can feel disappointed almost daily in the battles we lose.

However, we do not need to lose hope, because Jesus Christ is our victory over sin.

God, through Jesus Christ, acted on our behalf. He sent *His own Son in the likeness of sinful flesh to be a sin offering. And so He condemned sin in the flesh* (Romans 8:3-4). When we are made new in Christ, we are truly free from the condemnation of sin. Although we will continue to struggle for victory over our flesh here on earth, we do not have to live as though we are condemned forever by sin. If we do, we only discredit the power of what Christ accomplished for us on the cross, and we will weaken the power of the Spirit within us. Therefore, let us live victoriously through Christ, who has freed us from sin and counted us worthy to continue His work here on this earth. *Thanks be to God, who delivers [us] through Jesus Christ our Lord!* (Romans 7:25).

For in my inner being I delight in God's law; but I see another law at work in me, waging war against the law of my mind and making me a prisoner of the law of sin at work within me. Romans 7:22-23

What a wretched man I am! Who will rescue me from this body that is subject to death? Thanks be to God, who delivers me through Jesus Christ our Lord!
Romans 7:24-25

Therefore, there is now no condemnation for those who are in Christ Jesus, because through Christ Jesus the law of the Spirit who gives life has set you free from the law of sin and death. Romans 8:1-2

A LASTING CROWN

Everyone who competes in the games goes into strict training. They do it to get a crown that will not last, but we do it to get a crown that will last forever. Therefore I do not run like someone running aimlessly; I do not fight like a boxer beating the air. 1 Corinthians 9:25-26

THE WORLD IS filled with those who are running aimlessly toward crowns that do not last. This approach to life has become so common that no one even questions its validity. From a very young age, people are raised to set goals for themselves to become the best they can be, no matter the cost. To triumph above others and see the reflection of their own glory is what most people strive for. Inwardly, they are hoping this is where the meaning of life lies, for they have given it their all. After years of striving toward greatness, the crown is presented. However, the glory that illuminates their life lasts only for a few short moments.

What utter disappointment, therefore, is found in living to gain the trophies of this world, for earthly successes never deliver on the promises they whisper to one's heart. Instead, they are revealed for what they truly are: *meaningless, a chasing after the wind* (Ecclesiastes 1:14). Without eternal purpose, the toil of one's hands is in vain and *nothing [is] gained under the sun* (Ecclesiastes

2:11), except emptiness and despair. What a deceptive prize this is! Yet so many people shut their eyes to this truth, and in turn, make that which is meaningless the desire of their hearts. But we, as followers of Christ, are called to a different destiny.

We are called to *fight the good fight of faith* and *take hold of the eternal life to which [we] were called* (1 Timothy 6:12). Our crown is eternal, and our work here on earth is filled with purpose, for Christ never requires that we labor in vain. Every step He asks us to take contributes to the fulfillment of His redemptive plans for this broken and weary world. Unlike those with worldly roots, we do not have to speculate about the meaning of life because we know it resides in Christ. God's Spirit within us drives us toward our purpose and urges us to *press on toward the goal to win the prize for which God has called [us]* (Philippians 3:14). Praise God for the eternal victory we have in Jesus Christ!

But thanks be to God! He gives us the victory through our Lord Jesus Christ. 1 Corinthians 15:57

Their destiny is destruction, their god is their stomach, and their glory is in their shame. Their mind is set on earthly things. But our citizenship is in heaven. And we eagerly await a Savior from there, the Lord Jesus Christ. Philippians 3:19-20

Yet when I surveyed all that my hands had done and what I had toiled to achieve, everything was meaningless, a chasing after the wind; nothing was gained under the sun. Ecclesiastes 2:11

HIS MIGHTY FORCES

He said, "Do not be afraid, for those who are with us are more than those who are with them." 2 Kings 6:16

As CHRISTIANS, WE do not always embrace the command, "Do not be afraid." Instead, we feel quite the opposite: we feel afraid because we feel outnumbered. We look at our own communities and notice that only a fraction of our neighbors and friends claim allegiance to Christ. We turn on the world news to see the rise of evil people who proclaim their hatred of Christianity and anyone who supports it. From a numbers perspective, we see ourselves as the underdog who must take on a much larger beast. Like the servant of Elisha, we may anxiously proclaim, *Oh no, my lord! What shall we do?* (2 Kings 6:15).

The problem with this perspective, however, is that we are focusing only on the numbers we can see, and they are merely human numbers. Do we not believe that God has vastly supreme spiritual armies that are exceedingly greater than the forces of this world? The God who stands by our side is the one who *thunders at the head of His army* with forces that *are beyond number* (Joel 2:11). His legions are uncompromising in their purpose and unstoppable in the face of evil: *they charge like warriors; they scale walls like soldiers. They all march in line, not swerving from their course* (Joel 2:7). Whom shall we fear if this is the army of God?

As Elisha prayed for his servant, we too can pray this for ourselves: *open [our] eyes, Lord, that [we] may see* (2 Kings 6:17) the heavenly forces that are on our side. As we become aware of the power that surrounds us, we can let go of our fear and instead fix our eyes on the security we have in God Almighty. We do not have to hide in the darkness of anxiety when God desires for us to go forth as light into the world. We are His hands and feet on this earth, and we must go where He needs us: into the places of our communities and world where the light is dim. We may have to face some earthly giants and come up against those who side with the enemy, but as we step forward with purpose, we know that the greatest forces of good are on our side.

And Elisha prayed, "Open his eyes, Lord, so that he may see." Then the Lord opened the servant's eyes, and he looked and saw the hills full of horses and chariots of fire all around Elisha. 2 Kings 6:17

Do you think I cannot call on My Father, and He will at once put at My disposal more than twelve legions of angels? Matthew 26:53

The Lord is my light and my salvation—whom shall I fear? The Lord is the stronghold of my life—of whom shall I be afraid? Psalm 27:1

HIS ALL-SUFFICIENT POWER

Jesus replied, "They do not need to go away. You give them something to eat." "We have here only five loaves of bread and two fish," they answered. "Bring them here to Me," He said. Matthew 14:16-18

SOMETIMES GOD ASKS us to do things that only can be accomplished by His power. As Jesus was healing people and speaking to the crowds one day, He asked the disciples to take one small lunch and feed over 5,000 people with it. The disciples looked at what they had and saw how insufficient it was, yet Jesus asked them to bring it to Him anyway. As they placed what little they had into His hands, a miracle began. As Jesus thanked God for the food, it multiplied before their eyes, and *all ate and were satisfied* (Matthew 14:20).

Has God asked you to do something that seems virtually impossible? Has He asked you to face overwhelming odds or difficult circumstances? Perhaps, like the disciples, you can only see what little you have to offer. You look at your talents, skills, and abilities, and they seem so vastly inadequate compared to what you are facing. You may think, "How can something glorious be accomplished out of this?" But the beauty of our identity as followers of Christ is that we are not required to face these challenges on our own. We do not have to rely on our own strength, for we have the power of our savior Jesus Christ to draw upon, and it is all-sufficient and complete.

We simply must bring what little we have and place it into His mighty hands, asking Him to work powerfully and miraculously through us. We may be insufficient on our own, but with Christ on our side and the Holy Spirit living in us, we are more than sufficient. Every time God places a task in front of us that seems daunting, He is teaching us to embrace the truth that *what is impossible with man is possible with God* (Luke 18:27). He wants us to experience the victorious Christian life, a life lived through His power, not ours. He wants us to witness His ability to multiply our efforts for His glory and for the good of His people. No matter what we face, we can be certain that *all things are possible with God* (Mark 10:27).

Now to Him who is able to do immeasurably more than all we ask or imagine, according to His power that is at work within us, to Him be glory in the church and in Christ Jesus throughout all generations, for ever and ever! Amen.
Ephesians 3:20-21

For I can do everything through Christ, who gives me strength. Philippians 4:13

Such confidence we have through Christ before God. Not that we are competent in ourselves to claim anything for ourselves, but our competence comes from God.
2 Corinthians 3:4-5

IN SILENT SOVEREIGNTY

*For the L*ORD *has told me this: "I will watch quietly from My dwelling place—as quietly as the heat rises on a summer day, or as the morning dew forms during the harvest."* Isaiah 18:4 NLT

THE RISING HEAT of a summer day is silent, and the morning dew appears without notice. Quietly and consistently they come, in the time which is appointed. Likewise, God sits quietly in His dwelling place, gazing down upon us with a calm, watchful eye, not straining to see what is going on or worrying about what will take place. With the calm assurance only the Sovereign Lord can have, He sits patiently, waiting to work things out in His perfect timing. To us, the silence may seem empty and devoid of meaning, but God works with purpose each moment as He watches. Although He watches quietly, He is prepared to act swiftly at the appointed time.

Isaiah recorded the words of the Lord in chapter 18 as God's people were facing a battle with Cush, *a people feared far and wide* (Isaiah 18:2). As anxiety grew in the people's hearts, they most likely were filled with fear and desperation. However, we know that the Lord in heaven was not feeling the same. He sat quietly upon His throne, not threatened in the least by man's attempt to dominate and conquer the world in which He alone reigns. How miniscule their power must have appeared before God, who is able to *bring princes to naught and reduce the rulers of this world to nothing* (Isaiah 40:23).

At just the perfect time, God would *snip off and discard [the] spreading branches* of the enemy (Isaiah 18:5) of His people. And He will do the same for us today. If we stand faithful to Him, He will always act at the perfect time and in perfect purpose, for *we know that in all things God works for the good of those who love Him* (Romans 8:28). We may not understand the silence, but we can be assured that God knows its purpose. What we see as inactivity on God's part is actually His supernatural ability to withhold His hand until the greatest opportunity for victory. How grateful we can be that He is not like us—rash, impulsive, and impatient. He always sees the greater picture and never achieves anything but victory.

Humble yourselves, therefore, under God's mighty hand, that He may lift you up in due time. 1 Peter 5:6

Wait for the LORD; be strong and take heart and wait for the LORD. Psalm 27:14

With a mighty hand and outstretched arm; His love endures forever. Psalm 136:12

THE POWER OF WEAKNESS

The LORD turned to him and said, "Go in the strength you have and save Israel out of Midian's hand. Am I not sending you?" "Pardon me, my lord," Gideon replied, "but how can I save Israel? My clan is the weakest in Manasseh, and I am the least in my family."
Judges 6:14-15

THE FEAR IMPOSED by the ruthless Midianites, whose numbers were like locusts (Judges 6:5), only emphasized the weakness of the Israelite people. The Midianites lorded over them, devouring their crops and livestock, forcing the Israelites to hide out in caves and dens, living in fear. Among these fearful people was Gideon, and he was the very least of them. Yet one day, as Gideon was hiding in his family's winepress threshing wheat, an angel of the Lord made a shocking announcement to him. He declared, *The LORD is with you, mighty warrior* (Judges 6:12).

The term "mighty warrior" may have pierced Gideon's heart with guilt as he hid out in the winepress, avoiding the eyes of the enemy. However, God did not see him as simply weak and afraid. Instead, He saw in Gideon the very quality needed to become a vessel for His mighty power: human weakness. Through Gideon, God would prove that His *power is made perfect in weakness* (2 Corinthians 12:9), and that it requires no strength or strategy on the part of man. That day in the winepress, God chose exactly the right man to help save Israel. Because Gideon realized his own powerlessness, God's Spirit was able to take over and transform him into the man God had made him to be.

Becoming what God calls us to be always begins with humbly realizing how vastly inadequate we are without Him. It begins with recognizing that at the point of our weakness, God is the strongest. This is not always an easy task since our culture worships self-reliance and independence. However, in reality, those are the very things that can lead us away from God. Therefore, God, in His wisdom, sometimes chooses to display our inadequacies and weaknesses to our prideful hearts, so that we can be emptied of ourselves and instead filled with Him. It is at that point, when we feel very low and unworthy, that God will come to us and call us to do something great for His name. And we can be assured of His victory because His power is never greater than when we are at our weakest.

But we have this treasure in jars of clay to show that this all-surpassing power is from God and not from us.
2 Corinthians 4:7

For the foolishness of God is wiser than human wisdom, and the weakness of God is stronger than human strength. 1 Corinthians 1:25

But God chose the foolish things of the world to shame the wise; God chose the weak things of the world to shame the strong. 1 Corinthians 1:27

GIFT OF GRACE

Here is a trustworthy saying that deserves full acceptance: Christ Jesus came into the world to save sinners—of whom I am the worst. 1 Timothy 1:15

OUR LIVES OFFER no good reasons for God to love us and bless us with His grace. On the contrary, they often produce considerable evidence of our unfaithfulness toward Him, the One who created us and loves us. However, when it comes to fulfilling our own selfish desires, we stand faithful and true to ourselves! We have been *foolish, disobedient, deceived and enslaved by all kinds of passions and pleasures* (Titus 3:3). Yet, astoundingly, we are the ones whom Christ came to save. Without Him, we are bound to sin, desperate and needy, lost and hopeless. He alone is our saving grace. He takes the worst of sinners and says, "I love you, and I will make you new."

In my heart, I must ask of God: *What is mankind that You are mindful of them, human beings that You care for them?* (Psalm 8:4). Certainly, we have done nothing to deserve God's love or attention, for we are the worst of sinners, yet His unfailing love is what we get. Our minds cannot comprehend a love that is so pure and good that it graces us with mercy instead of condemnation, but that is what we receive. From our own human perspective, we believe that people should have to live with the consequences of their actions, for they are simply getting what they deserve. However, if we had to stand on our own good works ourselves, how low we would fall!

We can praise God, therefore, that He does not operate on the same human-based principles we use to judge others. Instead, He operates on the principle of grace: through *the kindness and love of God our Savior ... He saved us, not because of righteous things we had done, but because of His mercy* (Titus 3:4-5). Every blessing we have as the children of God comes simply because He has gifted it to us. We have not earned even a small portion of our salvation. Only through the sacrificial death of Christ have we gained *new birth into a living hope* and *an inheritance that can never perish, spoil or fade* (1 Peter 1:3). So when our flesh becomes prideful and we start viewing ourselves as righteous on our own account, may we remember that we are simply the sons and daughters of grace.

For it is by grace you have been saved, through faith--
and this is not from yourselves, it is the gift of God—not
by works, so that no one can boast.
Ephesians 2:8-9

This is love: not that we loved God, but that He loved us
and sent His Son as an atoning sacrifice for our sins.
1 John 4:10

Praise be to the God and Father of our Lord Jesus Christ!
In His great mercy He has given us new birth into a
living hope through the resurrection of Jesus Christ from
the dead, and into an inheritance that can never perish,
spoil, or fade. This inheritance is kept in heaven for you.
1 Peter 1:3-4

HIS STRENGTH IS OUR VICTORY

*Through You we push back our enemies; through
Your name we trample our foes.*
Psalm 44:5

GOD NEVER CALLS us to find strength in our own power.
To do so would be requiring the impossible. Instead,
He takes us, weak as we are, and supplies all the power
we need to carry out His plans on this earth. As we set
out to live a life of purpose for Christ, mere human
strength will not be sufficient to stand strong against the
forces that we will encounter. For our struggles are *not
against flesh and blood but ... against the powers of this
dark world and against the spiritual forces of evil in the
heavenly realms* (Ephesians 6:12). Our allegiance with
Christ is the reason such forces rise against us, but it is
also our greatest strength in conquering them.

From a human perspective, the opposing forces we
face may seem unconquerable, but they are no threat
if Christ is living in us. Certainly, Satan is relentless in
his attacks and strong in his power, but he is no match
for our Lord who conquered Satan in His victory on the
cross. Not even Satan's greatest threat, death, could keep
Christ down. And that *same mighty power that raised
Christ from the dead* (Ephesians 1:19-20) resides within
us if we believe in Him. God wisely prepares us with

spiritual weapons and armor, not physical ones, to *fight the good fight of the faith* (1 Timothy 6:12).

Unlike our enemy, we have the spiritual weapon of truth on our side. We also have the trusted Word of God and the saving power of the gospel message to combat the lies of the enemy. Above all, we have our own salvation as a guarantee of eternal victory. Undoubtedly, *we are more than conquerors through Him who loved us* (Romans 8:37). But we must intentionally put on our armor before we step out into battle; we cannot race ahead unequipped. Even when we think we know best and can fight our own battles, we are not strong enough to face our spiritual enemies alone. The power of Christ in us is the greatest gift we are given as believers. May we embrace it as we set out to gain victory in His name!

I also pray that you will understand the incredible greatness of God's power for us who believe Him. This is the same mighty power that raised Christ from the dead and seated Him in the place of honor at God's right hand in the heavenly realms. Ephesians 1:19-20

Therefore put on the full armor of God, so that when the day of evil comes, you may be able to stand your ground, and after you have done everything, to stand. Ephesians 6:13

Since the children have flesh and blood, He too shared in their humanity so that by His death He might break the power of him who holds the power of death—that is, the devil. Hebrews 2:14

IN THE QUIET PLACE

Be still before the Lord *and wait patiently for Him.*
Psalm 37:7

A MULTITUDE OF voices swirl around us, proclaiming, "Listen to me!" Wherever we are—in our homes, our workplaces, or our churches—there are many people demanding our listening ears. Even when we retreat to a closed room free from these voices, the noise does not seem to stop. As we sit down to quietly read our Bible or have a time of prayer, a vast number of thoughts come racing through our minds, trying to steal away the very moments we could dedicate to the Lord. The chaos and worries of our hurried lives penetrate the barriers of our minds, fighting against our need to *be still before the* Lord (Psalm 37:7).

We must not become a slave to these voices but instead, rebuke them. Just as Jesus quieted the violent, crashing waves of the sea with His voice, we must also say, *Quiet! Be still!* (Mark 4:39) to the competing voices within us. Only through the power of the Holy Spirit can this prayer be answered; we cannot conquer this alone. But God will be faithful to answer our prayers if we seek Him with a heart that is *fully committed to Him* (2 Chronicles 16:9). He will not hesitate to calm the storm within us and bring us the peace needed to hear

His quiet, gentle voice.

In this place of quietness before the Lord, we will be able to renew our minds and discern His direction. As we draw close to Him, we *will be able to test and approve what God's will is* (Romans 12:2), confirming His calling on our life. Only in our stillness, not in our striving, will God speak to us and reveal things we could never fully understand on our own. The deep things of God are whispered to our souls as we connect with Him on a very personal and profound level. It is here that our souls will find peace as God silences the clamoring voices of the world and offers us the peace of His presence and love.

Yes, my soul, find rest in God; my hope comes from Him.
Psalm 62:5

Do not conform to the pattern of this world, but be transformed by the renewing of your mind. Then you will be able to test and approve what God's will is—His good, pleasing and perfect will. Romans 12:2

This is what the Sovereign LORD, the Holy One of Israel, says: "In repentance and rest is your salvation, in quietness and trust is your strength." Isaiah 30:15

THE WORK OF HIS HANDS

The LORD will fulfill His purpose for me; Your steadfast love, O LORD, endures forever. Do not forsake the work of Your hands. Psalm 138:8 ESV

THE HANDS OF God are upon our lives, shaping and molding us into the people He has called us to be: people who will fulfill His purposes on this earth. Yet sometimes, our doubts can lead us to believe that He may not finish what He started. When we haven't seen our prayers answered or our purpose fully realized, we can begin to wonder if God has perhaps forgotten the plans He made for us. Instead of trusting in the faithfulness of God, we trust in the things we can see, and many times, we can find no evidence of our fruitfulness. However, that does not mean God isn't working in our lives at this very moment.

In Isaiah 55:8, God declares, *For My thoughts are not your thoughts, neither are your ways My ways.* Very rarely does God work in the exact timing and manner in which we think He will, for He sees and knows things we cannot even comprehend. This makes it quite difficult for us to predict the outcome of God's work in our lives, for we cannot visualize the intricate weavings of His greater plans. We are a part of them, but our role is not always clear and definable. We may think God is using us in one particular way, only to find out one day in eternity that He was using us in a multitude of ways we did not even realize.

Only God knows the plans He has for us (Jeremiah 29:11), and only He can *carry it on to completion* (Philippians 1:6) through the work of His hands. The Lord is faithful, and we can be assured that He will fulfill His purpose in our lives as we follow His leading. He never forsakes those He loves, nor makes plans that will harm them. He leads us in hope every day we walk with Him, and even when we cannot see it, He is guiding us with great purpose each step of the way. So even on those days when our eternal vision is clouded with earthly frustrations or confusion, we must hold even more tightly to the hand of God, knowing in full confidence that He will *never forsake the work of [His] hands.*

"For I know the plans I have for you," declares the Lord, *"plans to prosper you and not to harm you, plans to give you hope and a future."* Jeremiah 29:11

He who began a good work in you will carry it on to completion until the day of Christ Jesus. Philippians 1:6

Can you fathom the mysteries of God? Can you probe the limits of the Almighty? Job 11:7

OUR EYES ARE ON YOU

We do not know what to do, but we look to You.
2 Chronicles 20:12 HCSB

Has God brought you to this place? Has He allowed you to come to the end of yourself so that you realize the vast powerlessness of your own human strength and wisdom? In such a desperate place, the circumstances can seem daunting and overwhelming, while you feel so frail and inadequate. Yet what great hope there is when we view ourselves from such an honest perspective! Knowing we cannot conquer the giants around us alone, we are left with one option: to fix our eyes upon the only one who can truly save. As we focus on Him, our own helplessness fades away, and God's mighty power to save is displayed with such clarity before our eyes.

King Jehoshaphat of Judah was a man who knew where to fix his eyes when faced with an impossible situation. As enemy armies gathered to fight against his people, he could see no possible way out, yet he knew whom to turn to. In the face of his fear, *he resolved to seek the Lord* (2 Chronicles 20:3). He called his people to fast, and then gathered them together to pray before the Lord. The concluding words of his prayer are a humble plea to a mighty God: *For we are powerless before this vast number that comes to fight against us. We do not know what to do, but we look to You* (2 Chronicles 20:12).

There is no greater place to be than humble before the Lord with our eyes upon Him. Here God will eagerly answer our prayers, just as He did with Jehoshaphat. After Jehoshaphat's prayer, the Spirit of the Lord came down and spoke to the people of Judah: *Do not be afraid or discouraged because of this vast number, for the battle is not yours, but God's ... position yourselves, stand still, and see the salvation of the Lord* (2 Chronicles 20:15,17).

What amazing power there is when we stand in complete dependence upon the Lord! As He goes before us and fights the battle, we are safely tucked behind Him, shielded by the power that *no one can stand against* (2 Chronicles 20:6). The giants that once seemed so formidable become powerless before the Lord, and the hope that seemed so out of reach becomes reality before our eyes. This is the great blessing for those who turn their eyes away from their own strength and toward the One who has the power to save.

Yahweh, the God of our ancestors, are You not the God who is in heaven, and do You not rule over all the kingdoms of the nations? Power and might are in Your hand, and no one can stand against You.
2 Chronicles 20:6

If disaster comes on us—sword or judgment, pestilence or famine—we will stand before this temple and before You, for Your name is in this temple. We will cry out to You because of our distress, and You will hear and deliver.
2 Chronicles 20:9

The LORD *is the one who will go before you. He will be with you; He will not leave you or forsake you. Do not be afraid or discouraged.* Deuteronomy 31:8

THE RESULT OF BITTERNESS

*They angered the Lord at the waters of Meribah, and
Moses suffered because of them; for they embittered his
spirit, and he spoke rashly with his lips.*
Psalm 106:32-33 HCSB

IF WE ALLOW others to embitter us, we will surely suffer.
Bitterness, by nature, is like a root that grows up to
cause trouble and defile many (Hebrews 12:15). It easily
springs up in our hearts when we are surrounded by it.
The complaints and dissatisfaction of others can become
seeds of destruction within us, growing quickly and
abundantly, choking out everything good and making
a way for bitterness. Once it takes up residence in our
hearts, it is nearly impossible to restrain it from our lips.
And although it may feel satisfying to release our anger
to the ones who have caused it, we accomplish nothing
except to spread the bitterness further.

The root of bitterness had a devastating effect on
Moses, who dealt with the complaining and grumbling
of the Israelites for years in the wilderness. The people
quarreled with him, blamed him for all of their hardships,
and expressed their disbelief in God to him on a regular
basis. Moses had been extremely faithful to the Israelites,
but as they gathered against Aaron and him at Meribah,
claiming he brought them to the wilderness to die, he

became embittered. In response to their accusations, he proclaimed, *Listen, you rebels, must we bring you water out of this rock?* (Numbers 20:10). Then he struck the rock in anger, showing great dishonor to God.

Like Moses, we may have hearts dedicated to the Lord, but if we allow destructive attitudes to invade them, we will eventually dishonor God. Bitterness has a way of telling us that seeking revenge through words is a rightful course of action. It tells us that if someone causes us harm, we deserve to speak our own words of justice to them. However, these types of words only *defile a person* (Matthew 15:18) and dishonor the Lord. Because of Moses' harsh words, God did not allow him to enter the promised land; he could only gaze upon it from afar. We do not want to experience the same. God wants to lead us as far as He can into the promised land of our own journey; may we do nothing to deter His plans.

But the Lord said to Moses and Aaron, "Because you did not trust in Me enough to honor Me as holy in the sight of the Israelites, you will not bring this community into the land I give them." Numbers 20:12

A good man brings good things out of the good stored up in his heart, and an evil man brings evil things out of the evil stored up in his heart. For the mouth speaks what the heart is full of. Luke 6:45

Do not harden your hearts, as at Meribah, as on the day at Massah in the wilderness. Psalm 95:8

HOPE OF LIVING WATER

The LORD will guide you always; He will satisfy your needs in a sun-scorched land and will strengthen your frame. You will be like a well-watered garden, like a spring whose waters never fail. Isaiah 58:11

WE MAY LIVE in a land of spiritual poverty, but through our obedience to God, we can flourish in a dry and *sun-scorched land.* This is what sets us apart from the world around us. In the middle of a vast desert, we are to be *a well-watered garden,* a picture of hope to those who are desperately seeking to quench their eternal thirst. *Like a spring that never fails,* we have an everlasting source of power flowing through us, originating in Jesus Christ. To those who believe, Jesus declared that *rivers of living water will flow from within them* (John 7:38). This is the power of the Holy Spirit within us. Are we displaying His great power, or are we masking its brilliance?

Over time, many of us find that our lives have become withered and dry, producing less fruit each day as we dismiss the fact that such power resides within us. Without notice, we slowly begin to fade to the same shade of brown that covers the entire land, and the characteristic that once distinguished us from all others is no longer identifiable. Those seeking life and truth find no oasis to run to as their eyes scan the dry and thirsty land. When Christ walked the earth, He Himself was the living water, and He offered it to all. He proclaimed, *Let anyone who is thirsty come to Me and drink* (Matthew 7:37). People ran desperately to Him, and He met them at their place of greatest need.

Oh, that our lives could offer the same great hope—unashamedly and without reservation—to the generations today! Thankfully, we have a God who does not leave us wondering how to do this. To show His love and hope to others, He asks us *to loose the chains of injustice and untie the cords of the yoke, to set the oppressed free* (Isaiah 58:6). In a world filled with despair, we are to be to the lost and needy what no one else will be. That is how we will be set apart. As we let the *rivers of living water* flow through us, we can share the heart of Jesus with others, offering them the same great hope He provided when He walked this earth. In this day and age, we are called to be Christ's hands and feet. Let us offer them to all who will come.

And if you spend yourselves in behalf of the hungry and satisfy the needs of the oppressed, then your light will rise in the darkness, and your night will become like the noonday. Isaiah 58:10

On the last and greatest day of the festival, Jesus stood and said in a loud voice, "Let anyone who is thirsty come to Me and drink. Whoever believes in Me, as Scripture has said, rivers of living water will flow from within them." By this He meant the Spirit, whom those who believed in Him were later to receive.
John 7:37-39

Our people must learn to devote themselves to doing what is good, in order to provide for urgent needs and not live unproductive lives. Titus 3:14

SEEKING HIS FACE

My heart says of You, "Seek His face!"
Your face, LORD, I will seek.
Psalm 27:8

THE MORE WE know God, the more we want to seek His face. The more we dig deeply into His Word, the greater our desire is to understand the mysteries within it. In our lives, we have followed a thousand different pursuits born of the heart, but all have left us empty. Yet, as our heart cries out, *Seek His face,* it is left burning with a fire that will never die. When we wake up, our first thoughts are of Him, and when we lie down to sleep at night, our hearts still yearn for Him. God Himself is our reward, and all other desires fade into nothing before His greatness.

We seek God because He is our most valuable treasure, and we want to know the depth of His riches. Every moment of our lives offers us an opportunity to unearth the jewels of His heart and to store them up in ours. This is what kindles the fire in our hearts for Him; the treasures we find keep us seeking more. For *The Lord looks down from heaven on all mankind to see if there are any who understand, any who seek God* (Psalm 14:2), and He abundantly blesses those who do. These blessings are not earthly riches or worldly rewards; they are sacred gifts added to the storehouses of our hearts.

Such an overflow of God's goodness upon our lives is the cause of our joy and the reason we will never stop seeking Him. God *strengthen[s] those whose hearts are fully committed to Him* (2 Chronicles 16:9) and with joy, He will continue revealing to us the treasures of His heart. In Amos 4:5, God told His people, *Seek Me and live.* May we answer this great call on our lives as children of God. Only through seeking Him can we have true life! God Himself prompts our hearts to seek His face, and may we, His people, always respond, *Your face, Lord, I will seek!*

Glory in His holy name; let the hearts of those who seek the Lord rejoice. Look to the Lord and His strength; seek His face always. 1 Chronicles 16:10-11

From the rising of the sun to the place where it sets, the name of the Lord is to be praised. Psalm 113:3

For where your treasure is, there your heart will be also. Matthew 6:21

UNWAVERING FAITH

Yet he (Abraham) did not waver through unbelief
regarding the promise of God, but was strengthened in
his faith and gave glory to God, being fully persuaded
that God had power to do what He had promised.
Romans 4:20-21

ARE YOU LIVING in circumstances that seem to completely defy a promise that God made to you? Perhaps you *waver through unbelief* because your eyes can only see defeat, and your mind cannot imagine a possible road to victory. However, where you see a path filled with mountains of obstacles, God sees a straight path, for He is the one who can *go before you and ... level the mountains* (Isaiah 45:2). God is completely capable of accomplishing far beyond what we could ask for or imagine, but we ourselves must be *fully persuaded that God [has] power to do what He [has] promised.*

Abraham and Sarah's old age seemed to contradict the fact that they would have descendants as numerous as the stars, yet Abraham did not cease to believe that God could do what seemed humanly impossible. He placed all of his trust in the one *who gives life to the dead and calls into being things that were not* (Romans 4:17). Abraham knew that if God could create the universe from nothing, He could raise up a son from two aging people. Simply stated, *Abraham believed the Lord, and He credited it to him as righteousness* (Genesis 15:6). This is the type of faith that God will bless beyond measure, for He longs for His children to trust him and to believe He is who He says He is.

Unlike man, God *does not change like shifting shadows* (James 1:17) or swerve from His purposes. He doesn't claim to be faithful and then turn His back on the ones He loves. He stands steadfast and true, faithful *to a thousand generations of those who love [Him] and keep [His] commandments* (Exodus 20:6). His Word is our treasure, more valuable than gold, for *every word of God proves true* (Proverbs 30:5 NLT). Therefore, as His beloved children, we can take hold of His promises and consider them accomplished by the power of His Word. Even when our worldly perspective tells us we are facing the impossible, we can trust in the Word of God, which tells us that *with God all things are possible* (Matthew 19:26).

Is anything too hard for the LORD? I will return to you at the appointed time next year, and Sarah will have a son.
Genesis 18:14

And without faith it is impossible to please God, because anyone who comes to Him must believe that He exists and that He rewards those who earnestly seek Him.
Hebrews 11:6

I will go before you and will level the mountains; I will break down gates of bronze and cut through bars of iron.
Isaiah 45:2

CHILDREN OF LIGHT

*I have hidden Your Word in my heart that
I might not sin against You.*
Psalm 119:11

THE CONSTANT LURE of sin waits at the door of our hearts, and it will do anything to enter. Without any defense in place, it most certainly will creep in and have its way in our lives. The lies that sin offers us can be so alluring, and our minds are quick to produce a multitude of justifications for any sinful action we may take. In our selfishness, we close our ears to the Spirit of God within us and open them up to the lies of the enemy. This is dangerous ground for all Christians, and we must *be careful that [we] don't fall* (1 Corinthians 10:12).

Therefore, let us fortify our defenses against sin by storing God's words in our hearts. Let us fill ourselves up with words that are *full of the Spirit and life* (John 6:63) so that God's light will reside within us. Then, as sin wages war against us—children of light—we will be able to lift *the sword of the Spirit, which is the Word of God* and *take [our] stand against the devil's schemes* (Ephesians 6:17,11). We will engage in battle against a tenacious enemy, but we will not fall, for the light of God's Word can never be overcome by the darkness of Satan. Jesus Christ Himself guaranteed this victory when He conquered death on the cross, and as believers, we carry that same hope within us as we fill ourselves up with the *light of life* (John 8:12).

Although we are not perfect like our savior, Christ offers us greater victory over sin each day as we become stronger and stronger in His Word, enabling us to more effectively draw the sword of the Spirit. As we engage in God's Word, our light will grow brighter and we will be able to clearly see the ugliness of sin, for *everything exposed by the light becomes visible* (Ephesians 5:13). The ugly truth of sin will send us running in the opposite direction, and it will prompt our hearts to yearn for the true light of our heavenly home. However, until that day comes, we must keep strengthening ourselves to fight off the darkness of this world, so that we can be what God has called us to be: the children of light.

For you were once darkness, but now you are light in the Lord. Live as children of light. Ephesians 5:8

When Jesus spoke again to the people, He said, "I am the light of the world. Whoever follows Me will never walk in darkness, but will have the light of life." John 8:12

In Him was life, and that life was the light of all mankind. The light shines in the darkness, and the darkness has not overcome it. John 1:4-5

HEAVENLY ROAD

And a highway will be there; it will be called the Way of Holiness; it will be for those who walk on that Way. The unclean will not journey on it; wicked fools will not go about on it. Isaiah 35:8

As BELIEVERS IN Christ, our souls yearn for a heavenly road. Even with the blessings of peace and joy that God places in our hearts, we realize that we are foreigners and strangers on earth (Hebrews 11:13). As we travel down the highways of this earth with the road stretching out endlessly before us, we long for a place that is beyond the horizon, for a place that truly feels like home. We want to search this earth to find it, but in our hearts we know the destination will not be found here, for our citizenship is in heaven (Philippians 3:20) and our Savior resides there.

Jesus Christ Himself is *the way and the truth and the life* (John 14:6), and He leads us in everlasting ways even as we are here on this earth. Yet one day, we will experience the heavenly kingdom of God firsthand, pure and undefiled by this world, as God had intended it to be. Christ our Savior will triumphantly lead us on the Way of Holiness *to the city of the living God ... to the church of the firstborn, whose names are written in heaven* (Hebrews 12:22-23). In this place, our longing for a true home will be ultimately fulfilled as we praise our faithful God with *thousands upon thousands of angels in joyful assembly* (Hebrews 12:22). Our minds cannot even fathom such joy. How eternally blessed are the ones *who walk on that Way!*

As those who love Christ, our hearts may long to be *away from the body and at home with the Lord* (2 Corinthians 5:8), but we can serve Him faithfully wherever we are. Just as Christ was given an appointed time on this earth, we too are called to fulfill the plans God has for us in our current generation. Eternity will reign forever, but the present time will not. Our time is short, and all around us is a sea of people whose hearts are seeking the very thing we have already found: peace through Jesus Christ. As recipients of such grace, what greater gift can we offer than to guide as many of them as possible to the *road that leads to life* (Matthew 7:14)? In our hearts, we may long to be with our Lord, but our Lord desires that we bring more hearts to Him. May His will be done.

For while we are in this tent, we groan and are burdened, because we do not wish to be unclothed but to be clothed instead with our heavenly dwelling, so that what is mortal may be swallowed up by life. 2 Corinthians 5:4

We are confident, I say, and would prefer to be away from the body and at home with the Lord. So we make it our goal to please Him, whether we are at home in the body or away from it.
2 Corinthians 5:8-9

But small is the gate and narrow the road that leads to life, and only a few find it. Matthew 7:14

A FIRM PLACE TO STAND

He lifted me out of the slimy pit, out of the mud and mire; He set my feet on a rock and gave me a firm place to stand. Psalm 40:2

THE PROBLEM WITH being in a pit is that no mere human can reach you there. The depths are too profound and the darkness too black for anyone to lift you out. Although you may look pleadingly to those above you, all they can do is gaze helplessly down at you. However, there is one whose arms can reach effortlessly to infinite depths and whose heart yearns to save the ones He loves. Through countless generations He has been faithful to those who have cried out to Him from unreachable places, where troubles surround and sin overwhelms (Psalm 40:12 paraphrased).

Our God is our deliverer, and nothing can stop Him when He is determined to save. The mud and mire have no effect on His ability to rescue us, nor do they deter Him from wanting to draw near to us. In His great love and desire to save us, He meets us wherever we are—for even darkness does not affect Him. He lifts us out of the ruins and sets us on solid ground, removing the stains of our lives with such complete forgiveness that our sins become *as white as snow* (Isaiah 1:18). The waves of grace that wash over us at such a transformation spark a new *hymn of praise to our God* (Psalm 40:3) within our hearts. It refreshes our spirit and brings renewed energy to follow Him unashamedly with our whole heart.

By freeing us from our pit of selfishness and destruction, God brings us to the point where we can earnestly declare, *Here I am, I have come ... I desire to do Your will, my God; Your law is in my heart* (Psalm 40:7). When we start desiring His will over our own, we know we are walking closer to Him and further away from the trap of the pit. Our hearts begin to yearn for Him alone as we realize that He Himself is our great reward, and a life devoted to Him is what we long for most. He can give us no greater gift than a heart transformed closer to His likeness and a life given to His cause. The redeemed life is the beginning of true living.

For troubles without number surround me; my sins have overtaken me, and I cannot see. They are more than the hairs of my head, and my heart fails within me. Be pleased to save me, LORD; come quickly, LORD, to help me.
Psalm 40:12-13

Surely the arm of the LORD is not too short to save, nor His ear too dull to hear. Isaiah 59:1

But may all who seek You rejoice and be glad in You; may those who long for Your saving help always say, "The LORD is great!" Psalm 40:16

AT THE FEET OF JESUS

She had a sister called Mary, who sat at the Lord's feet listening to what He said. But Martha was distracted by all the preparations that had to be made. "Martha, Martha," the Lord answered, "you are worried and upset about many things, but few things are needed—or indeed only one. Mary has chosen what is better, and it will not be taken away from her." Luke 10:39-42

COME, SIT AT the feet of Jesus and listen to Him, even when the pressing responsibilities of life urge you away. Set aside the weight of your own agenda and the endless obligations that try to steal each moment away, and present Jesus with the offering of your time. How gladly He will receive it, and how refreshed you will be as His peace rushes over the worries of your heart. Nothing in this world can strengthen our souls like the quiet moments with Jesus, when His words become strength to us and His presence settles upon us. When we choose Jesus over the distractions of this world, we, like Mary, have chosen what is better and it will not be taken away *from [us]* (Luke 10:42).

The world offers only that which is temporary, calling us to work tediously for *food that spoils* (John 6:27) and riches that fade. However, what Christ offers is *food that endures to eternal life* (John 6:27). When we sit enraptured at His words, absorbing their life-giving nature, we build in our hearts a treasury of the eternal. And as these infinite riches grow, we become more keenly aware of the futility of striving to accomplish endless tasks. Like Mary, we need not be *worried and upset about many things* because there is truly only one thing that matters.

The one thing we need is what Jesus recognized in Mary: a willingness to sit down amidst the chaos and listen to His voice. Like Mary, if we choose to shut out all of the competing voices of this world for His voice alone, we will greatly bless the heart of God, and He, in turn, will bless ours. The sacrifice of our time and attention is a rare gift offered to God in a world of busyness and distractions, and He will honor us for our decision. The rewards He gives will not be temporary like the trophies of this world, which will rust and be forgotten, but instead will be everlasting. God alone will give us what the world can never offer: joy in our hearts and peace in our souls.

Do not work for food that spoils, but for food that endures to eternal life, which the Son of Man will give you. For on Him God the Father has placed His seal of approval. John 6:27

Then they asked Him, "What must we do to do the works God requires?" Jesus answered, "The work of God is this: to believe in the one He has sent."
John 6:28-29

Come to Me, all you who are weary and burdened, and I will give you rest. Take My yoke upon you and learn from Me, for I am gentle and humble in heart, and you will find rest for your souls. Matthew 11:28-29

ABUNDANCE

"Bring the whole tithe into the storehouse, that there may be food in My house. Test Me in this," says the LORD Almighty, "and see if I will not throw open the floodgates of heaven and pour out so much blessing that there will not be room enough to store it." Malachi 3:10

LET US GIVE back to God what is rightfully His and watch as His abundant blessings flow. Just as we are called to honor the Lord with [our] wealth, with the firstfruits of all of [our] crops (Proverbs 3:9), we are also called to bring Him the full tithe of our lives. The best of who we are belongs to the Lord, for He made us new through the blood of Jesus Christ and we are His. Therefore, the greatest gifts we can offer Him are the firstfruits of our lives, and nothing less. In honoring God this way, we prompt God to unleash the floodgates of heaven and pour down blessings beyond measure.

When we bring Him our best, we are simply responding to Him in obedience. God rarely asks us to test Him, yet when it comes to honoring Him through our obedience, that is what He asks of us. He challenges us to simply obey His commands, bringing all we have to offer, so that He can amaze us with *showers of blessings* (Ezekiel 34:26) from His heavenly storehouse. Certainly, what we bring to the Lord cannot compare to what He gives in return, yet how priceless our obedience must be that He should reward it so greatly!

In a world where so many choose to bring God only the remnants of their life's work, a life devoted fully to God must be a rare blessing to Him indeed. It is no wonder that God would choose to display His heavenly riches so abundantly to those who are willing to bring the full tithe of their lives before Him. To see His children lay down their lives for His cause must stir images of His Son's life work on this earth, a picture of complete submission and obedience to His will. Therefore, is there anything greater we can offer God than to live according to the ways of Christ? Our complete devotion will be the highest honor to God and a testimony to His Son. May our lives forever bless the Lord.

I will make them and the places surrounding My hill a blessing. I will send down showers in season; there will be showers of blessing. Ezekiel 34:26

Honor the LORD with your wealth,
with the firstfruits of all your crops.
Proverbs 3:9

I know, my God, that You test the heart and are pleased with integrity. All these things I have given willingly and with honest intent. And now I have seen with joy how willingly Your people who are here have given to You.
1 Chronicles 29:17

FAITH IN THE STORM

But now I urge you to keep up your courage, because not one of you will be lost; only the ship will be destroyed ... So keep up your courage, men, for I have faith in God that it will happen just as He told me. Acts 27:22, 25-26

GOD WILL BRING you safely to your destination, although He may not lead you on the route you had hoped for. Smooth sailing is not always the path God uses to get His children to the places where He calls them to be, yet He is faithful to bring them through. Even when our ship is battered beyond repair, and we are forced to swim to the shore through turbulent waters, God Himself will carry us along and *[draw us] out of deep waters* (2 Samuel 22:17). As He sets us upon the shore, we may be exhausted, but we will have renewed faith in the unstoppable nature of His plans for our lives.

For Paul, the destination was Rome, and he knew God's plans for His life would not be thwarted. An angel appeared to Him on the storm-battered ship and said, *Do not be afraid, Paul. You must stand trial before Caesar* (Acts 27:24). Nothing Paul would encounter—not even the darkest storm where *neither sun nor stars appeared for many days* (Acts 27:20)—would hinder the perfect timing of his arrival in Rome. Because Paul trusted fully in the Word of God, he had a confidence throughout the storm that defied all logic. With absolute certainty, he knew everyone on the ship would soon be standing safely on the shore. On a ship filled with fear, Paul was instead filled with the grace of God, and he gave hope to those around him, urging them *to keep up [their] courage.*

Perhaps it is for this same reason that we are often called to travel down roads of suffering and trials, so that the grace of God may be apparent to all who are watching. Maybe the light of our hope, which shines even in the darkest storms, will bring the courage and hope of Jesus to those who desperately need it. Most certainly, God could quiet the raging storms in our lives with just the sound of His voice; however, quiet waters do not always bring Him the greatest glory. God will never let go of the divine plans He has for us, yet He may require that we step off the path of comfort and ease for the sake of those around us. Through our trials, God may be building the faith of others, but most certainly, He is building ours.

These have come so that the proven genuineness of your faith—of greater worth than gold, which perishes even though refined by fire—may result in praise, glory and honor when Jesus Christ is revealed. 1 Peter 1:7

Last night an angel of the God to whom I belong and whom I serve stood beside me and said, "Do not be afraid, Paul. You must stand trial before Caesar; and God has graciously given you the lives of all who sail with you." Acts 27:23-24

He reached down from on high and took hold of me; He drew me out of deep waters. 2 Samuel 22:17

A MATTER OF POWER

For the kingdom of God is not a matter of talk but of power. 1 Corinthians 4:20

SOMETIMES GOD PRESSES down upon our hearts, urging us to seek more from His Word. Although we may adore Scripture and esteem it highly with our brothers and sisters in Christ, God desires that His Word be the driving force of power in our lives. He wants to move us from being mere spectators and analysts of His Word to participants who embrace a life that functions on His full power. God's kingdom is built upon His holy words, and they *will never pass away* (Matthew 24:35), but if we never embrace their life-changing power, His words will ring hollow in our hearts.

The words in the Bible are not merely words etched across a white page; they are an invitation to come face to face with the power of God. No other book can make such an offer. When we read the Bible, we absorb the breath of God from its sacred pages, and if we are willing, His words can change us. If we allow ourselves to sit and be still before the Lord, praying that He will open our eyes to understand His Scripture (Luke 24:45), we will find Him more than willing to deliver. He will bring the power of His words to the forefront of our vision and then etch their truths deeply within our hearts.

From the inside out, God will transform us through His mighty power. He will allow us to see that the evidence of our faith is not found in our ability to speak eloquently about the Word of God; instead, it is displayed through the testimony of a changed life. Our lives will cease to be full of powerless talk, and instead, we will become proof that God's kingdom *is not a matter of talk but of power.* A transformed life that defies all human logic is one God can use for His glory, and it is one He can use to draw others toward Him. May we allow the power of God's words to change us into who He wants us to be—for the sake of His name and the spread of His fame.

My message and my preaching were not with wise and persuasive words, but with a demonstration of the Spirit's power, so that your faith might not rest on human wisdom, but on God's power. 1 Corinthians 2:4

All Scripture is God-breathed and is useful for teaching, rebuking, correcting and training in righteousness. 2 Timothy 3:16

Heaven and earth will pass away, but My words will never pass away. Matthew 24:35

GIFT OF ENCOURAGEMENT

*The brothers and sisters there had heard that we were
coming, and they traveled as far as the Forum of Appius
and the Three Taverns to meet us. At the sight of these
people Paul thanked God and was encouraged.*
Acts 28:15

WHAT JOY AND thankfulness floods our hearts at
the sight of other believers in Christ! We may feel
outnumbered in this world, but the faces of our brothers
and sisters in Christ can renew our downtrodden spirit
like nothing else can. Simply seeing them can give us
the encouragement we need and the strength to press
on. We are bonded together with an eternal tie, one that
only believers in Jesus Christ can experience as members
of His family. Christ stated that *whoever does the will of
My Father in heaven is My brother and sister and mother*
(Matthew 12:50). Therefore, even though Christ cannot
physically be with us, He has blessed us with spiritual
siblings to encourage us in our faith.

How greatly Paul must have rejoiced each time he
was greeted by believers in the cities he traveled to. To
Paul, these believers were an extension of God's love
that he could lay his eyes upon and put his arms around.
They were an offering of God's love poured out to him
in a real, tangible way. God knew that the road Paul was

traveling could be lonely and filled with despair, so He gave him the blessing of others to show him that he truly was not alone. Paul knew that God was always with him, and surely he would have persevered through God's strength alone, but his joy was made complete through the encouragement of his brothers and sisters in Christ.

Like Paul, our joy, too, will abound if we share our lives with other believers. Most certainly, the Christian life was never meant to be lived alone, for our strength lies in each other. Contrary to a life of isolation that only serves to build up walls around a person's heart, a life lived in community brings our hearts together, strengthening us beyond our own individual abilities and multiplying our joy. Just as laughter is never enjoyed as much alone as with others, the joy of our faith will never be fully realized in solitude. Sharing the common bond of our faith with fellow believers is the key to experiencing a foretaste of our future with Christ. Most certainly, when we reach our heavenly home, we will be praising our Savior together, and we will be as one.

The glory that You have given Me I have given to them, that they may be one even as We are one, I in them and You in Me, that they may become perfectly one, so that the world may know that You sent Me and loved them even as You loved Me. John 17:22-23

And let us consider how we may spur one another on toward love and good deeds, not giving up meeting together, as some are in the habit of doing, but encouraging one another—and all the more as you see the Day approaching. Hebrews 10:24-25

He replied to him, "Who is My mother, and who are My brothers?" Pointing to His disciples, He said, "Here are My mother and My brothers. For whoever does the will of My Father in heaven is My brother and sister and mother." Matthew 12:48-50

DEEP THINGS OF GOD

The Spirit searches all things, even the deep things of God. 1 Corinthians 2:10

THERE ARE NO substitutes for the *deep things of God*. Yet when we turn away from the leading of God's Spirit, we tend to gravitate toward the shallow things of the world. Our hearts and minds can be easily convinced that our innermost needs can be met by searching out a vast range of worldly options. We believe that perhaps the answer to our yearning lies in finding the perfect soul mate, experiencing the excitement of a trip to a far-off destination, or advancing our careers for great financial gain. All such things tempt us to believe the answer to our longings is out there somewhere, if we just keep searching diligently.

A problem arises, however, when we acquire all of those things for ourselves and still have the same unfulfilled yearning in our soul. Or, on the contrary, we are never able to acquire them and realize our searching has been in vain. Either way, we are left empty, faced with the undeniable truth that the deep things we have been searching for lie only within God. How foolish we can feel after years of such vain toil through which we ignored the promptings of God in order to follow our own plans. Yet what abundant proof they offer to the superiority of a life controlled by the Holy Spirit! Indeed, our souls long to go deeper, and only God can take us there.

As children of God saved through Jesus Christ, *we have the mind of Christ* (1 Corinthians 2:16), and it is satisfied with nothing less than the deep and hidden things of God. Only through His Word and His Spirit will we find the treasures that our souls so desperately seek. We must open our hearts and minds to Him, seeking Him diligently as if searching for treasure. And unlike our futile searching in the world, we do not have to wonder where the treasure lies. God has given us His Spirit, *so that we may understand what God has freely given us* (1 Corinthians 2:12), and He wants to fill us to the point of overflowing. We do not have to live on the crumbs of satisfaction that the world offers—we can be filled with His incomparable riches.

Indeed, if you call out for insight and cry aloud for understanding, and if you look for it as for silver and search for it as for hidden treasure, then you will understand the fear of the LORD and find the knowledge of God. Proverbs 2:3-5

My goal is that they may be encouraged in heart and united in love, so that they may have the full riches of complete understanding, in order that they may know the mystery of God, namely, Christ, in whom are hidden all the treasures of wisdom and knowledge.
Colossians 2:2-3

What we have received is not the spirit of the world, but the Spirit who is from God, so that we may understand what God has freely given us. 1 Corinthians 2:12

A PURE HEART

And you, my son Solomon, acknowledge the God of your father, and serve Him with wholehearted devotion and with a willing mind, for the Lord searches every heart and understands every desire and every thought.
1 Chronicles 28:9

WHAT IF GOD gathered up the secret things of our hearts and placed them before our eyes? Would we be surprised at what we saw? The Lord Himself knows *every desire and every thought* in our hearts, yet sometimes we do not even recognize them ourselves. Perhaps, more accurately, we do not want to be confronted with the true intentions of our selfish hearts, so we press them down deeper to avoid the conflict that arises within us. Over time, our hearts can slowly become hardened and inaccessible, for fear of revealing too much. However, God, in His great love for us, desires that we reveal all to Him so He can make us clean.

King David, the father of Solomon, knew from his own experience how important *wholehearted devotion* to the Lord would be for his son, the next king of Israel. David himself experienced a time when sinful motives captured his heart and drew him away from the Lord, turning a heart that beat powerfully for the Lord into one that became inaccessible to Him. Like many of us, he ignored the Lord's promptings and chose to follow his own self-serving motives. However, when God opened his eyes to the reality of his sin, he wisely cried out, *Create in me a pure heart, O God, and renew a steadfast spirit within me* (Psalm 51:10).

God will always answer such a desperate prayer from a God-seeking heart. With joy, He will *remove from [us our] heart of stone and give [us] a heart of flesh* (Ezekiel 36:26). The substance of our hearts will no longer have to be hidden because they will overflow with goodness and joy. Just as David experienced, we will be able to stand unashamed in the presence of the Lord once more. A transformed heart does wonders for our souls, but it also blesses the heart of God. Christ said that *the pure in heart ... will see God* (Matthew 5:8). This blessing appears to be ours alone, yet how greatly we will bless the Lord as we stand pure in His presence, hearts devoted to Him alone.

Who shall ascend the hill of the LORD? And who shall stand in His holy place? He who has clean hands and a pure heart, who does not lift up his soul to what is false.
Psalm 24:3-4

Blessed are the pure in heart, for they will see God.
Matthew 5:8

I will give you a new heart and put a new spirit in you; I will remove from you your heart of stone and give you a heart of flesh. Ezekiel 36:26

KING OF GRACE

One who loves a pure heart and who speaks with grace
will have the king for a friend. Proverbs 22:11

WHEN KING SOLOMON penned these words, could he
have imagined just how clearly they would illustrate
our relationship with our Savior and King, Jesus Christ?
Could he have known what a cherished and faithful
friend we would have in Jesus? Certainly, he held the
perspective of a God-appointed king, but I wonder if
he could grasp the incomparable grace that the coming
Messiah would offer to the world. Solomon knew
what kind of friend best suited a king, but Jesus Christ
Himself became that friend to us so He could draw us in
with His grace and lovingkindness. Through His grace,
He has saved us, and through our transformed hearts,
we become His friends.

God has blessed us with *grace upon grace* (John
1:16) through the glory of His one and only Son. God
did not send His Son to the world to condemn it, but to
save it (John 3:17), and His loving arms want to reach
out and save us all. Our God is not some distant deity
who looks down upon us with feigned interest; He is
the greatest friend we will ever know. He will carry us
during the darkest days of our lives, when no one else
even knows we are hurting, and revive us with the gift

of His unconditional love. He will hold fast to us during the depths of our depravity, never condemning us, but instead blanketing us with such grace and kindness that it leads to our repentance. How unworthy we are, yet what a faithful friend we have in Jesus!

The blessings we receive from Jesus become the overflow of our own hearts, and the words of grace we speak and the acts of kindness we display become evidence of our allegiance to the one true king. We are able to bless others through Him *so that the grace that is reaching more and more people may cause thanksgiving to overflow to the glory of God* (2 Corinthians 4:15). Nothing about God's love and grace is ordinary, nor is it limited by boundaries. He is the God who overflows with spiritual riches as He pursues the ones He loves, *not wanting anyone to perish, but everyone to come to repentance* (2 Peter 3:9). We are the loves of His life, and He demonstrated that on the cross when He laid down His life for us, His friends. May our lives continue His legacy of grace!

> *Greater love has no one than this: to*
> *lay down one's life for one's friends.*
> John 15:13

> *I no longer call you servants, because a servant does not*
> *know his master's business. Instead, I have called you*
> *friends, for everything that I learned from My Father I*
> *have made known to you.* John 15:15

> *But when the kindness and love of God our Savior*
> *appeared, He saved us, not because of righteous things*
> *we had done, but because of His mercy.* Titus 3:4-5

LIMITS OF UNBELIEF

And He did not do many mighty works there, because of their unbelief. Matthew 13:58 ESV

WHEN WE BELIEVE we cannot do something God has called us to do, we set up a roadblock against the very thing we need to complete the task—God's power! Our unbelief becomes the reason that God does not perform mighty works in our lives. Since our strength is tied directly to our estimation of God's power, our lack of faith can greatly hinder His willingness to carry out the plans He has for us. Just as Jesus did not perform many miracles in places that met Him with unbelief, God will not release His full power to an unbelieving heart.

Many of us are like the father whose boy was possessed by an evil spirit (Mark 9:14-29). We seek out God because He is our only hope, yet we approach Him as if we are just taking our chances. We come to God with little faith, just like the unbelieving father who told Jesus, *If You can do anything, take pity on us and help us.* In dismay, Jesus replied, *If You can?* (Mark 9:23). How astounded the Son of God must be when we present such skeptical requests to Him, the guardian of limitless power. For certainly, through Him *everything is possible for one who believes* (Mark 9:23).

Perhaps our first step is to simply cry out to Jesus that

we need help overcoming our unbelief. The father of the possessed boy exclaimed, *I do believe; help me overcome my unbelief!* (Mark 9:24). Although he desperately wanted to believe, he recognized that his heart was full of skepticism. If we struggle in a similar way, we too are free to come before God with an honest heart, conflicted as it is, and admit our unbelief. God will not reject us because of our honesty; instead, He will find ways to build up our faith. Just as He miraculously released the father's son from the grip of an evil spirit, He will also be eager to show us just how worthy He is of our trust. And perhaps then, we will begin to witness *many mighty works* in our lives.

"You deaf and mute spirit," He said, "I command you, come out of him and never enter him again." The spirit shrieked, convulsed him violently and came out.
Mark 9:25-26

See to it, brothers and sisters, that none of you has a sinful, unbelieving heart that turns away from the living God. Hebrews 3:12

And Jesus said to them, "A prophet is not without honor, except in his hometown and among his relatives and in his own household." And He could do no mighty work there, except that He laid His hands on a few sick people and healed them. And He marveled because of their unbelief. Mark 6:5-6 (ESV)

POWER TO RUN

The power of the LORD came on Elijah and, tucking his cloak into his belt, he ran ahead of Ahab all the way to Jezreel. 1 Kings 18:46

SOMETIMES GOD CALLS us to sit quietly and wait upon Him, yet at other times He empowers us to act. As with Elijah, we have no choice but to get up and run when God's power falls upon us. The Holy Spirit drives us to accomplish His purposes, no matter how great the distance or how difficult the terrain. Although weak on our own, we become unstoppable in the face of overwhelming odds, enabled by God's ability to grant us His unlimited power. Elijah was able to outrun a chariot for nearly twenty miles, not because he was a gifted runner, but because the strength of the Lord drove him forward.

Still today, God sets His undaunted Spirit within believers to accomplish His purposes. Some of His plans may appear to exceed our capabilities, but God will achieve them through His own strength if we believe He can. Elijah certainly believed in the power of God's spirit. Through it, he brought a boy back to life and called down fire from heaven to swallow up a drenched altar. He personally experienced God's supernatural victory over earthly impossibilities and knew there were no limits to what God could do. Therefore, when God's power came upon him to run to Jezreel, he did not hesitate to *[tuck] his cloak into his belt [and run]*.

Like Elijah, we can step out in faith, for we know we are traveling down the right road if the Spirit of the Lord is with us. When we feel a supernatural power taking the helm of our lives, driving us to do His will, we can be assured we are heading in the right direction. With God in control, we can have a confidence we have never had before, for it is founded in the sovereign, almighty Lord, not in ourselves. We are able to *run with perseverance the race marked out for us* (Hebrews 12:1), for surely God will help us run it. If we simply step forward in obedience, He will set our feet in motion and keep fueling us along the way with the power of His Spirit.

Let us throw off everything that hinders and the sin that so easily entangles. And let us run with perseverance the race marked out for us. Hebrews 12:1

Then he stretched himself out on the boy three times and cried out to the LORD, "LORD my God, let this boy's life return to him!" The LORD heard Elijah's cry, and the boy's life returned to him, and he lived. 1 Kings 17:21-22

Then the fire of the LORD fell and burned up the sacrifice, the wood, the stones and the soil, and also licked up the water in the trench. When all the people saw this, they fell prostrate and cried, "The LORD—he is God! The LORD—he is God!" 1 Kings 18:38-39

FAITHFUL AND TRUE

*I saw heaven standing open and there before me was
a white horse, whose rider is called Faithful and True.
With justice He judges and wages war ... On His robe
and on His thigh He has this name written: King of kings
and Lord of lords.* Revelation 19:11,16

OUR SOULS LONG for the ultimate victory that only
Jesus Christ can bring. How deeply our hearts yearn to
see our Savior riding forth mightily on His white horse,
demanding the justice that for so long has been delayed. To
watch the rider called Faithful and True striding steadily
and fearlessly toward the greatest enemy of humanity will
be a breathtaking sight to behold. Most assuredly, we will
be there, for as Scripture states, when Jesus Christ comes
to fight the final battle against His enemy, with Him will
be His called, chosen and faithful followers (Revelation
17:14). Even at this climactic event of God's great plan,
Christ stands faithful and true to His followers, wanting
us to share in a victory that in truth is His alone to claim.

This is a remarkable testament to the exceedingly great
and honorable nature of Jesus Christ's kingship. The title,
King of kings and Lord of lords, is rightly engraved upon the
fibers of His being, for no other king throughout the span
of time could match the heart He has for His people. Only
Christ, our noble king, would come to this earth to endure

scorn and suffering at the hands of man, sacrifice Himself for them, and then allow His chosen ones to share in the victory He already accomplished through His own blood. The majesty and wonder of who He is lies beyond our comprehension, and only when we see His glory revealed before our very eyes will we understand His greatness.

Until that day, we can honor Him with a faith that is completely abandoned to Him, preparing our hearts for an eternity of singular adoration toward Him. He alone is worthy to be praised, and every moment of our eternal life will display that truth vividly. Yet in the here and now, we must do all we can to *prepare the way for the Lord* (Isaiah 40:3), to ready mankind for the day when Christ will return and His judgment will be made final. Just as John the Baptist prepared a *straight path* (Mark 1:3) for Jesus Christ on this earth, we too can ready people for His ultimate return. In a land full of spiritually thirsty people, we can be *a voice of one calling in the wilderness* (Mark 1:3), offering a cup of living water to anyone who would come. How anxiously we await the arrival of our Savior, yet until that day, let us prepare the way for our Lord!

"I will send my messenger ahead of you, who will prepare your way"—"a voice of one calling in the wilderness, 'Prepare the way for the Lord, make straight paths for Him.'" Mark 1:2

A voice of one calling: "In the wilderness prepare the way for the Lord; make straight in the desert a highway for our God." Isaiah 40:3

They will wage war against the Lamb, but the Lamb will triumph over them because He is Lord of lords and King of kings—and with Him will be His called, chosen and faithful followers. Revelation 17:14

UNSTOPPABLE

*But Jews came from Antioch and Iconium, and
having persuaded the crowds, they stoned Paul and
dragged him out of the city, supposing that he was dead.
But when the disciples gathered about him, he rose up
and entered the city.*
Acts 14:19-20

RISE UP! WALK back onto the path God has chosen for you, no matter what lies ahead. Satan wants to claim victory through our suffering, yet God desires to produce great glory from it. We are already assured victory, for Jesus Christ Himself conquered our greatest enemy, freeing us from the power of fear and death. Our job as followers of Christ is to never stop believing that His power is ours and that He will forever lead us triumphantly over the ways of this world. We know, as Paul did, that *we must go through many hardships to enter the kingdom of God* (Acts 14:22), but if we remain faithful to Him, we will be able to accomplish His will, even against all odds.

As Paul walked back into the city that had nearly killed him, he became a living picture of the unstoppable nature of God's plans and purposes. He proved that even in the face of the enemy, God can accomplish His will through the life of a faithful believer. Angry mobs wanted to silence Paul and the gospel message, but God wanted him to proclaim it loudly and without shame—so that is exactly what Paul did. Even the stones thrown by the hands of evil men could not stop him. They may have silenced him for a moment, but through God's power, he rose up from the brink of death and walked back onto the path God had destined him for.

That same power that breathed life back into Paul's stone-battered body resides in us today. Do we believe it? Can we confidently declare to God from the depths of our souls, *No purpose of Yours can be thwarted!* (Job 42:2)? The more faithfully we serve God, the more fully we understand the absolute truth of that statement. God is relentless, and His plans will be brought to completion. We can stand on the sidelines and observe, or we can step out with purpose to do His will, encompassed by the sovereignty of a faithful God. We have nothing to fear when we *entrust [our] souls to a faithful Creator* (1 Peter 4:19). Opposition may arise, but *it is the Lord's purpose that prevails* (Proverbs 19:21).

For the LORD Almighty has purposed, and who can thwart Him? His hand is stretched out, and who can turn it back? Isaiah 14:27

But the plans of the LORD stand firm forever, the purposes of His heart through all generations.
Psalm 33:11

Therefore let those who suffer according to God's will entrust their souls to a faithful Creator while doing good.
1 Peter 4:19

FREEDOM OF FORGIVENESS

I have swept away your offenses like a cloud,
your sins like the morning mist. Return to Me,
for I have redeemed you. Isaiah 44:22

ALTHOUGH GOD IS willing to *sweep away [our] offenses like a cloud*, we are often determined to live under the dark cloud of sin as retribution for what we have done. Though forgiven, we live as though the heavy weight of sin is still upon us. We believe that we should have to pay a price for what we have done in order to make the forgiveness of our sins truly complete. In our minds, a free pardon seems too good to be true, and we want to work for it like we do most other things in life. However, our desire to reconcile our own sin is far from the reality of God's complete and perfect forgiveness through Jesus Christ, His Son.

God views the forgiveness of our sins as an honor to His Son who paid the heavy price for them. Jesus Christ promised forgiveness to all who would repent, and God honors His Son when He grants us freedom from our sins. The blood of Jesus was a tremendously costly sacrifice, and its payment for our sin never loses its value, especially through the eyes of the Father who gave up *His one and only Son* (John 3:16). God wants all glory to go to His Son, and we can honor Him by seeking forgiveness as it truly is: a completed work of mercy and grace won through the precious blood of Jesus. We dishonor God by making it anything less.

Surely God knows our human inclination to hang on to the guilt of our sin, but He wants us to cling to His promises instead. We must believe Him when He says, *Come now, let us settle the matter ... though your sins are like scarlet, they shall be as white as snow* (Isaiah 1:18). It is done; forgiveness is complete. We do not have to hide in our own shame and guilt any longer, for we are pure in His eyes, renewed through the love and sacrifice of Jesus Christ. God calls out to us, *Return to Me, for I have redeemed you!* In essence, He urges us to believe that His forgiveness is enough for us to come running back to His arms. We are His children, and He loves us; we do not have to cower in shame before Him. Instead, we can rejoice in a Father who *remembers [our] sins no more* (Isaiah 43:25).

I, even I, am He who blots out your transgressions, for My own sake, and remembers your sins no more.
Isaiah 43:25

Let the wicked forsake their ways and the unrighteous their thoughts. Let them turn to the LORD, and He will have mercy on them, and to our God, for He will freely pardon. Isaiah 55:7

Repent, then, and turn to God, so that your sins may be wiped out, that times of refreshing may come from the Lord. Acts 3:19

A TIMELESS PURPOSE

Your eyes saw my unformed body; all the days ordained
for me were written in Your book before one of them
came to be. Psalm 139:16

DO YOU FEEL lost in a vast sea of people who seem more accomplished, confident, and successful than you? Do you tend to overlook all of your God-given abilities and instead focus on the things you are not? For many of us, our own insecurity becomes the shaky foundation of our identity. We cower away from the marvelous plans God has for us because we see ourselves as ordinary people who will never do anything extraordinary. We think greatness is something people are born with, and from our perspective, we do not qualify. We let our own self-criticisms, along with the opinions of others, determine who we are. Yet God knows us as we truly are.

God is the author of our lives, the one who ordained our days long before we were even formed. Before we even entered the scene of life, He filled us with a purpose that only we can fulfill. Contrary to our own faulty thinking, God did not *knit [us] together* (Psalm 139:13) with His own skillful and loving hands so that we would live a mundane, meaningless existence. No, He *fearfully and wonderfully made* (Psalm 139:14) us so that our life stories could be written across the generations in His great script of glory. What praise we should offer to God for allowing us to participate in such amazing work! Far from being insignificant, we are filled with His power and purpose.

When we start to doubt that such things are true, we must turn to God's Word to ponder the precious, unchanging thoughts of God. Then we will be able to shut out the incessant criticisms of man and the nagging voice of our own insecurity, and simply be still in the power of His presence. As we let His vastly superior thoughts settle upon us, our minds become renewed with a purpose that reaches far beyond our own imagination. The limits we set upon ourselves begin to fade away as we realize that the God who made us is the one who will lead us through every step of this life. Through His divine authorship, *He marked out [our] appointed times in history* (Acts 17:26), and now is our time. May God's glory reach the earth through us, His appointed ones in this generation!

From one man He made all the nations, that they should inhabit the whole earth; and He marked out their appointed times in history and the boundaries of their lands. Acts 17:26

For You created my inmost being; You knit me together in my mother's womb. I praise You because I am fearfully and wonderfully made; Your works are wonderful, I know that full well. Psalm 139:13-14

"For My thoughts are not your thoughts, neither are your ways My ways," declares the Lord. "As the heavens are higher than the earth, so are My ways higher than your ways and My thoughts than your thoughts." Isaiah 55:8-9

UNSHAKEABLE MOUNTAIN

Those who trust in the Lord are like Mount Zion, which cannot be shaken but endures forever. Psalm 125:1

Strong and secure are we as believers in Christ, like the foundations of Mount Zion where God's beloved city sits. Jerusalem, the city of David, from which God promised David a *throne [that] will be established forever* (2 Samuel 7:16), is a living memorial to a sovereign God whose plans and purposes cannot be shaken. Just as Jerusalem has been established as *a tent that will not be moved, [whose] stakes will never be pulled up* (Isaiah 33:20), we too, as believers in Jesus Christ, stand solidly upon the rock of our salvation. No matter what destructive winds blow across the landscape of our lives, the security of our souls will remain untouched.

God is our ultimate protector and His presence is our shield. Just *as the mountains surround Jerusalem, so the Lord surrounds His people both now and forevermore* (Psalm 125:2). In the valley of His protection, God keeps us eternally safe from anything that might rise up against us. He *[hems us] in behind and before* (Psalm 139:5), providing no way in for the enemy. And standing guard over us is Jesus Christ, our gentle yet mighty shepherd, who promises that *no one will snatch [us] out of [his] hand* (John 10:28). The fear that grips so many people in the world should not be ours. For in Christ, we find the peace and security that the whole world is seeking.

If we trust in the Lord, we will not be moved by the circumstances that threaten to steal our peace. We can plant our feet firmly on Mount Zion, making God *the sure foundation of [our] times* (Isaiah 33:6), so that we will endure with Him forever. The circumstances of our lives may continue to ebb and flow between great heights and depths, but our trust in the Lord is the one thing that can never be touched. *God is our rock and our salvation; He is our fortress, we will not be shaken (Psalm 62:6)!*

He will be great and will be called the Son of the Most High. The Lord God will give Him the throne of His father David, and He will reign over Jacob's descendants forever; His kingdom will never end. Luke 1:32-33

Look on Zion, the city of our festivals; your eyes will see Jerusalem, a peaceful abode, a tent that will not be moved; its stakes will never be pulled up, nor any of its ropes broken. Isaiah 33:20

The LORD is exalted, for He dwells on high; He will fill Zion with his justice and righteousness. He will be the sure foundation for your times, a rich store of salvation and wisdom and knowledge; the fear of the LORD is the key to this treasure. Isaiah 33:5-6

PERFECTED

Shall we accept good from God, and not trouble?
Job 2:10

WHAT IF WE knew our troubles and afflictions would result in glory for God and salvation for others? Would we be more willing to endure them? It is certainly not our natural reaction to want to embrace difficulties; in fact, we usually plead with God to remove them from our lives. But in asking Him to do so, is it possible we are asking Him to diminish the effect our lives will have on His kingdom plans? Perhaps the difficulties we so desperately pray for God to remove are actually the tools He is using to shape us into who He desires us to be.

Most often, God refines His children through *the furnace of affliction* (Isaiah 48:10), not through a life of ease and comfort. If our lives are going to be a testimony to His great power, we must have the experience of drawing upon it so that others can witness it. Just like a clay pot, we must allow ourselves to be molded by the hand of God to become exactly who He wants us to be. We may not understand why He has to etch so deeply into certain places of our lives, while He simply smooths out others, but we can trust that He knows best, for *we are all the work of [his] hand* (Isaiah 64:8). Each stroke He makes is an imprint of His purpose upon our lives.

Knowing we have a Maker who always desires what is best for us, we can look through all of the suffering and difficulty in our lives to foresee a Christlike image in the mirror. As God is shaping us through our afflictions, He is refining us to be more like His Son. Most certainly, Christ was perfected through His own suffering *as the pioneer of [our] salvation* in order to *[bring] many sons and daughters to glory* (Hebrews 2:10). Just as the kingdom of God grew through Christ's suffering, our lives too can bring growth to His kingdom. It may require suffering, but God will transform our character and turn our suffering into fruitfulness.

For those God foreknew He also predestined to be conformed to the image of His Son, that He might be the firstborn among many brothers and sisters. Romans 8:29

In bringing many sons and daughters to glory, it was fitting that God, for whom and through whom everything exists, should make the pioneer of their salvation perfect through what He suffered.
Hebrews 2:10

Yet You, LORD, are our Father.
We are the clay, You are the potter;
we are all the work of Your hand. Isaiah 64:8

OUTSIDE THE CAMP

And so Jesus also suffered outside the city gate to make the people holy through His own blood. Let us, then, go to Him outside the camp, bearing the disgrace He bore. For here we do not have an enduring city, but we are looking for the city that is to come. Hebrews 13:12-14

OUR PLACE IN this world is not within its gates but outside of them. Just as Christ was rejected by man and forced outside the city walls to suffer and die, we too must live on the edge of this world, for we *do not conform to the pattern of this world* (Romans 12:2). If we did, the world would love us and welcome us, but it does not. Instead, we dwell on the outskirts of the city, living as strangers on this earth, one foot planted on the soil of this land and the other stepping out toward our true home: *the city that is to come.*

Jesus Christ said of His followers, *they are not of the world any more than I am of the world* (John 17:14). Even when we find ourselves as misfits in a sea of people who all seem to fit together, we know that Christ went before us, and we can praise God that He has set us apart in the same way. We have been called out of this world in order to *declare the praises of Him who called [us] out of darkness into His wonderful light* (1 Peter 2:9). And although some days we may be tempted to seek the acclaim and approval of the world, our purpose is to shine light into its darkness as Christ's current ambassadors on earth.

When Jesus Christ came to earth as a light in a dark world, He was rejected because the people of the world chose *darkness instead of light* (John 3:19). He was ultimately cast out of the city, scorned by the ones He came to save, an outsider in the world He had created. However, *outside the camp,* His greatest work of salvation was made complete through the shedding of His blood, and He became a light to the entire world. We too can do our greatest work for Christ as we set ourselves apart from this world, yet lovingly embrace the people who so desperately need His light. Through His power, we can be a beacon of hope in a dark and sin-stained world.

If you belonged to the world, it would love you as its own. As it is, you do not belong to the world, but I have chosen you out of the world. That is why the world hates you. John 15:19

But you are a chosen people, a royal priesthood, a holy nation, God's special possession, that you may declare the praises of Him who called you out of darkness into His wonderful light.
1 Peter 2:9

He was in the world, and the world was made through Him, yet the world did not know Him. He came to that which was His own, but His own did not receive Him.
John 1:10-11

BROKEN

My people have committed two sins: They have forsaken
Me, the spring of living water, and have dug their
own cisterns, broken cisterns that cannot hold water.
Jeremiah 2:13

HOW FOOLISH OUR efforts must appear to God when we set out to dig cisterns next to *the spring of living water.* With closed eyes and a misled heart, we gather our tools and form our own plans to seek out the very thing God has already given us. But because our hearts have been deceived, we believe we can unearth something better ourselves. We dig and dig, exhausting ourselves in order to produce something that fulfills our aching souls, yet we end up with something vastly inferior to what God offers. In essence, we attempt to collect rainwater in a cistern when we could be drinking from the spring of living water.

When we give up the glory of God for things that are essentially worthless, God declares, *Be appalled at this, you heavens, and shudder with great horror* (Jeremiah 2:12). Although we may not see our wayward actions as appalling, God certainly does. He has granted us an immeasurable gift: to know and be known by Him, the true and living God. He has placed his unwavering love upon us and has set us apart as children of His everlasting kingdom. Therefore, when we turn to anything else to fulfill us, we reject the heart of God, declaring that He is not enough.

We will find ourselves broken and dismayed when we reject all the good that God has planned for us in exchange for the cheap work of our own hands. Furthermore, we will break the heart of God who has blessed us with His faithful love. Just as our hearts yearn for loyal and faithful love, God's heart does too, for He is not without feeling or emotion. Certainly, He is unwavering in His character and purpose, but He also has a heart that can feel the repercussions of giving Himself fully to His people. He knows there will be rejection, but He considers us worth the cost. Do we consider Him worth it? If we do, we can honor Him by offering Him nothing less than our pure, undefiled love. We can trade in the broken cisterns of our own hands for the eternal *spring of living water.*

You will joyfully draw water from the springs of salvation. Isaiah 12:3 HCSB

"Consider then and realize how evil and bitter it is for you when you forsake the Lord your God and have no awe of Me," declares the Lord, the Lord Almighty. Jeremiah 2:19

Do not turn away after useless idols. They can do you no good, nor can they rescue you, because they are useless. 1 Samuel 12:21

THE CONFLICT WITHIN US

Help, LORD, for no one is faithful anymore; those who are loyal have vanished from the human race. Psalm 12:1

A SPIRIT OF defeat can settle upon us as we walk out into a world that disregards the truth of Jesus Christ. When we leave the confines of our quiet place with the Lord and step out into a spiritually barren land, the contrast can be quite jarring to our senses. The power produced by praying and reading God's Word can dwindle all too quickly when we come face to face with masses of people who are largely apathetic, or even hostile, toward Jesus Christ, our Savior. The waves of unbelief that come crashing around us send our minds spinning as we try to merge the two different worlds into one.

Most certainly, we are not of this world, just as Jesus Christ was not (John 17:16), yet we are living right in the middle of it. As we transition from the moments we spend alone with God to the moments we step out into the world, we feel somewhat shocked by its godlessness, and the more we grow in our love and knowledge of our Savior, the harder it is to reconcile the two starkly different atmospheres. Our souls and this world were not made to be eternally matched, and the result within us can be a mix of both despair and longing. We yearn for a heavenly land our feet have never touched, feeling homesick on this earth.

Jesus Christ Himself experienced this same inner conflict, only on a much greater scale. He left heaven's glory, the land of our longing, to come and dwell with us on earth. As His godly feet stepped upon the soil of this earth, the purity of holiness met the depravity of sin, and the contrasts were as opposite as night and day. On certain occasions, He even expressed the conflict in His own heart. In Matthew 17:17, He declares, *"You unbelieving and perverse generation ... how long shall I stay with you?"* He longed for his true home, yet He persevered in love, staying with that *unbelieving and perverse generation* until His work on the cross was complete and hope was made available to all. May Christ be our greatest example as we step out in our own generation, persevering in the love of our Savior.

Praise be to the God and Father of our Lord Jesus Christ! In His great mercy He has given us new birth into a living hope through the resurrection of Jesus Christ from the dead. 1 Peter 1:3

For this world is not our permanent home; we are looking forward to a home yet to come. Hebrews 13:14

They are not of the world, even as I am not of it. John 17:16

ON THE EDGE OF IMPOSSIBLE

As Pharaoh approached, the Israelites looked up, and there were the Egyptians, marching after them. They were terrified and cried out to the Lord. Exodus 14:10

THAT DAY AT the edge of the Red Sea, the Israelites came face to face with the impossible. As they looked out over the vast sea and then back again to the Egyptians who were descending upon them, they saw nothing but sheer hopelessness and felt nothing but pure fear. As they clung desperately to their children, they cried out to Moses, asking why he had led them out to such a place to die. However, that day, at the edge of their desperation, God was getting ready to perform a mighty miracle, one that would save their lives. And on that day, the people of God would learn without a doubt what a mighty deliverer they had on their side. They would learn that absolutely nothing was impossible with Him.

At the edge of the water, Moses stood before the people and declared, *Do not be afraid. Stand firm and you will see the deliverance the Lord will bring you today. For the Egyptians whom you see today, you shall never see again.* (Exodus 14:13). At that moment, God brought forth His incomparable power and opened up the waters in front of them, providing a path of deliverance that they never could have imagined. As they passed through the towering walls of water with their feet treading upon dry ground, what awe and wonder must have gripped their hearts. Once again, God had shattered the limitations they had set upon Him.

Just like the Israelites, we have a hard time comprehending what great power God has over our lives until we are able to witness it for ourselves. For this reason, God sometimes chooses to take us to the edge of the impossible, to the places where we know we cannot make it on our own and we must rely on Him alone. And although we may experience fear, it is in these moments that He astounds us with His mighty power to save, driving us to our knees in awe and thankfulness for the kind of Savior He is. A life free from struggles would never help us arrive at the place where our faith is strengthened and our hearts are drawn closer to Him. Only through the dark, desperate situations of our lives can His faithfulness be fully revealed to us. Yes, sometimes God does take us *through the sea* and *through the great waters* (Psalm 77:19 ESV), but He takes us there so we can become the people He has called us to be.

Your way was through the sea, Your path through the great waters; yet Your footprints were unseen. You led Your people like a flock by the hand of Moses and Aaron.
Psalm 77:19-20 ESV

The LORD your God is with you, the Mighty Warrior who saves. Zephaniah 3:17

Jesus looked at them and said, "With man this is impossible, but with God all things are possible."
Matthew 19:26

THE IDOL OF HUMAN PRAISE

For they loved human praise more than praise from God.
John 12:43

WHEN THE DESIRE of our hearts is to gain the praise of others, we join the rest of the world in glorifying that which is meaningless. As we crave the adoration of man, and not of God, our lives become evidence that *what is worthless is exalted by the human race* (Psalm 12:8 HCSB). We love the sound of our own name followed by words of praise lifted up toward it, but its reward is fleeting, and most often the words ring hollow. *The heart is deceitful above all things* (Jeremiah 17:9), and it persuades us to believe that our worth comes from man, not from God.

When we demand that our value be determined by other flawed, imperfect people just like ourselves, we are standing on shaky ground. Our lives become a rollercoaster ride of emotions, based upon the whims and judgments of those we are trying to please. Some days, we soar high on the wings of praise, yet on others, we sink low in the depths of our unworthiness. We become slaves to an unfit master, who rarely has our best interests at heart and always demands more than we can give. When we bow to the idol of human praise, we choose to submit ourselves to ones who were never meant to be our masters.

In His great wisdom, God tells us to *stop trusting in mere humans, who have but breath in their nostrils. They do not have the power to save or redeem us. Why hold them in esteem?* (Isaiah 2:22). God was created to be our master, and *in his hand is the life of every creature and the breath of all mankind* (Job 12:10). The One who fashioned us with His hands is the only One who can satisfy our longing for true love and acceptance. Only He can lead us away from the false comfort of human praise and restore our lives with His pure joy and adoration. What a worthy master we choose to serve when we allow our heavenly Father to replace the empty idols of this world.

I said to the LORD, "You are my Master! Every good thing I have comes from You." Psalm 16:2 NLT

This is what the LORD says: "Cursed is the one who trusts in man, who draws strength from mere flesh and whose heart turns away from the LORD."
Jeremiah 17:5

How can you believe since you accept glory from one another but do not seek the glory that comes from the only God? John 5:44

THE SERENITY OF A SOUL

Yet I will rejoice in the LORD, I will be joyful in God my Savior. Habakkuk 3:18

DURING THE DARKEST days of our lives, the glory of God is revealed the most brilliantly. We may have longed for nothing but happiness and endless success, but had that come to fruition, we would have lost out on so much. The wonders of our God would have escaped us, and a nominal life of worldly success would have been our highest hope. The precious grace of Jesus would have been something to theorize about, not something to boast about from the depths of our souls. The blood-stained cross would have simply been an image of Christ's sacrifice instead of a place where we fall on our knees, overwhelmed by the absolute necessity of His redemption.

What riches the Father pours upon us as He draws us to Him out of the depths of our own deficiency! A life of attaining all of our desires could never lead us to such goodness. When we come to Him broken, He welcomes us with loving arms wide open, ready to take the shattered pieces of our lives and create something beautiful from them. We become the evidence of a God who performs miracles, and the touch of His hand is our greatest reward. Never could the riches of the world come close to competing with such brilliant, innocent joy! The highest earthly prominence is no match for the breathtaking moments in which we experience the overwhelming presence of a God who loves us and has chosen us out for His own.

A road free of suffering would never lead us to the places where God's glory is most fully revealed. It is in the deep, dark valleys that His light shines most brightly, illuminating our hearts and minds with the supreme knowledge that there is no better road than *the way and the truth and the life* (John 14:6). Only through the grace of Jesus are we driven to seek His heart above all else and dig deep into His Word. The treasury of His words becomes a lifeline to our souls, and His purposes become the essence of who we are. As we wrap ourselves up in the blanket of His sovereignty, embracing all of the wondrous plans He has for us, there is a serenity within us that no trial or hardship can touch. Praise be to God who makes all things well with our souls! There is none other like Him.

There is no one holy like the Lord; there is no one besides You; there is no Rock like our God.
1 Samuel 2:2

Jesus answered, "I am the way and the truth and the life. No one comes to the Father except through Me."
John 14:6

Your Word is a lamp for my feet, a light on my path.
Psalm 119:105

42730262R00075

Made in the USA
Middletown, DE
20 April 2017